Praise for Paul Meshanko and The Respect Effect

"Having worked with Paul and seen first-hand how he can take a room full of strangers and by the end of the session have a room full of respectful colleagues willing to go the extra mile for anyone in that room is amazing to watch. This book brings together those techniques and expands them to be applicable to any organization around the world. As we become a global economy, understanding respect is going to be the competitive advantage that will move a company from good to best in class."

—*Fernando Serpa, director, Global Diversity and Inclusion, Johnson Controls*

"Paul Meshanko does an outstanding job of simplifying significantly complicated neuroscience and positive psychology constructs and is able to connect them in a manner that will help businesses understand how to use their existing assets, cultivate them, build capacity from that effort while capitalizing on context and create a healthier and more sustainable eco-system for success. The book is applicable to multiple disciplines and crosses gender and cultural boundaries. Mr. Meshanko provides the tools and examples necessary to reach the key characteristics of what will make an individual or organization successful if they understand the respect effect."

—*Gina Weisblat, PhD College of Medicine, Dean's Office, Director of Education for Service, Assistant Professor Family/Community Medicine, National Kresge Scholar 2011–2013, Northeast Ohio Medical University*

"Truly a guidebook worth the respect it deserves, written in a stellar display of thoughtful counsel. For so many, respect must be learned before it can be earned. Aretha Franklin could spell it, Paul is spelling it out with clarity."

—*Daniel Moneypenny, president and CCO, Emaginit*

"Businesses aspiring to be a leader in their marketplace will find invaluable guidance in *The Respect Effect: Using the Science of Neuroleadership to Inspire a More Loyal and Productive Workplace*, by Paul Meshanko. In this accessible, engaging and thoughtful book, Meshanko eloquently articulates how neuroscience provides powerful new insights into why respect boosts employee engagement and performance. This is a must read for anyone interested in attracting and retaining the talent required to ensure sustainable business success."

—*Erica Pinsky, CHRP, author,* Road to Respect: Path to Profit

"In *The Respect Effect*, Paul describes the impact of a respectful work environment in a way that is logical and compelling to business leaders at all levels. Regardless of company size, industry, geographic location, we strive to create organizations that deliver strong business results and outstanding customer experiences through our people. To do this we often get caught up in the 'program of the day.' Paul reminds us that we already know much of what it takes build strong companies: know your employees as people, build their confidence, appreciate their contributions, make sure your actions match your words. His advice makes sense and his work is timeless."

—*Alan Jaffa, CEO, Safeguard Properties*

"Paul Meshanko challenges leaders to keep respect front and center of their employee engagement strategies. He combines common sense human relations with the science of brain function to propel the reader to take the necessary steps to master respectful behavior."

—*Daniel J. Woods, president and CEO,*
St. Anthony's Memorial Hospital

"Paul takes the concept of respect and turns in into a powerful leadership tool for the business world. By first proving respect's power, economically and psychologically, he lays a foundation for his potent cultural change tools. His blueprint for success is sharp and relevant, and of course, starts with respect for ourselves."

—*Dr. Stephen G. Payne, president, Leadership Strategies,*
Princeton, NJ

"Paul walks the talk. Whether you read his book or see him speak at a conference."

—*Hal Becker, author,* Can I Have 5 Minutes of Your Time;
Lip Service; *and* Get What You Want

"Paul Meshanko's analytical approach and insight to the importance of respect, particularly in the workplace is spot on. *The Respect Effect,* takes a deep dive into the brain's response to respectfulness but also shares real world examples of rock star companies that see and appreciate the power of respect. This is great validation for professionals who now have a quantifiable, metric-driven guide to support what they already felt to be true."

—*Jim Knight, former Sr. Director of Training and Development,*
Hard Rock International

"I believe in respect in the workplace. In fact, it is key to successful organizations. Paul Meshanko's book, *The Respect Effect* does an excellent job of concretely describing why it is so critically important."

—*Joe McAleese, president and CEO, Bendix*
Commercial Vehicle Systems LLC

"Paul Meshanko has focused on a critical but frequently overlooked aspect of leadership behavior. How to lead and engage people with respect to maximize individual and team performance. His message is very relevant in today's world of global business growth and cross border economies. Paul's focus on respect is helpful not just with employees, but with business colleagues, customers and in our personal life as well."

—*Timothy G. Beatty, vice president, Customer and*
Product Support, Honeywell Aerospace

The Respect Effect

The Respect Effect

Using the Science of Neuroleadership to Inspire a More Loyal and Productive Workplace

Paul Meshanko

New York   Chicago   San Francisco   Athens
London   Madrid   Mexico City   New Delhi
Singapore   Sydney   Toronto

1 2 3 4 5 6 7 8 9 0   DOC/DOC   1 9 8 7 6 5 4 3

ISBN   978-0-07-181609-0
MHID   0-07-181609-7

e-ISBN   978-0-07-181610-6
e-MHID   0-07-181610-0

Library of Congress Cataloging-in-Publication Data

Meshanko, Paul.
    The respect effect: using the science of neuroleadership to inspire a more loyal and productive workplace/Paul Meshanko.
        pages cm.
    ISBN-13: 978-0-07-181609-0 (alk. paper)
    ISBN-10: 0-07-181609-7 (alk. paper)
    1. Leadership.   2. Respect.   I. Title.
    HD57.7.M483 2013
    658.4'092—dc23   2013008353

McGraw-Hill Education books are available at special quantity discounts to use as premiums and sales promotions or for use in corporate training programs. To contact a representative, please visit the Contact Us pages at www.mhprofessional.com.

This book is printed on acid-free paper.

Contents

Preface

Inspiration comes from many sources. I give my mother credit for my natural and never-ending curiosity about people and relationships. When she was working on her master's degree in theology when I was in high school, I vividly remember endless conversations with her, sometimes late into the evenings, about religious belief systems, "truths," and what happens when different belief systems collide. Combine that with my personal love of philosophy, business, and neuroscience, and you have an interesting mix.

I was fortunate to be mentored by some amazingly intelligent and insightful adults outside my family. One person deserves special mention. In my sophomore year of college, I was elected president of my dorm council. The dorm director was a man named Dale Linder. Dale was an African American man, about six years my senior, and he possessed the wisdom of someone far older. To say that Dale and I clashed at times would be an understatement. Like many 20-year-olds, I had the mistaken notion that I was omnipotent; I was physically indestructible, had the world all figured out, and knew exactly where I was going in life. In my ignorance, I sometimes said and did things that today make me cringe when I think back. While my specific recollection of details may be a little sketchy, I do remember Dale saying to me on multiple occasions, usually after a sigh, "Paul Meshanko, you don't know what you don't know." He was right.

When it came to dealing with people, I felt we should look past each others' differences and treat everyone the same. You know, as in the Golden Rule. I tried to put on my rose-colored glasses and pretend that we could make stereotypes, prejudices, and social inequities go away just by wishing it so. I truly didn't know what I didn't know, and worse, I wasn't about to listen to anyone who suggested otherwise, including Dale. I still remember him, looking at me with a combination of frustration and determination, begging me to open my mind. He would say, "Paul, we're not all the same. If you won't acknowledge our differences and what those might mean, then you can't really respect me." Usually, my feelings would be hurt; I would get defensive and continue to insist that differences, like race, really didn't matter. In retrospect, it was my behaviors and attitudes that were hurtful. By intentionally failing to acknowledge Dale's blackness and other differences, I was treating him with disrespect.

I think it's that way with many of us. Through a combination of unintentional (sometimes purposeful) ignorance, competing agendas, and stubbornness, we make our way through life, sometimes treating others with disrespect along the way. The problem is that when people feel disrespected, they don't give us their best. They don't give us their attention, finest thinking, and utmost effort. Fortunately, Dale had seen people like me before and demonstrated a wisdom and graciousness that at times I didn't deserve. No matter how contentious our conversations, he would always wrap up by saying, "Paul, if I didn't push you, it would mean that I didn't care about you. But I do. I care about you deeply, and I want you to be successful in life." We should all be fortunate to have people like Dale in our lives because at some point we all demonstrate how much we really don't know.

While neither of us could have known it at the time, those long and sometimes heated conversations with Dale planted the seeds that would eventually sprout and grow into a career and calling that I love more each day. Because of the respect with which Dale and others treated me, I graduated from college not only with a degree, but with a sense of confidence, self-esteem, and humility.

I had confidence in my thinking and ability to be a life-long learner. I learned to honor myself and be steadfast in my belief that, whatever I ended up doing in life, it would add value to this world. Most importantly, I learned humility and developed a curiosity to explore the many blind spots that would eventually, and continuously, be brought to my attention.

When I think back to my experiences with Dale, I remember the movie *Avatar* and the line where the Na-vi acknowledged each other by saying, "I see you." Dale helped me see him as a unique individual. By seeing others as they are, black, white, short, tall, Asian, Indian, old or young, docile or angry, we acknowledge them and all that makes them unique. Only through discovering and acknowledging what they are can we genuinely understand and respect who they are.

Acknowledgments

Anyone who has ever gone through the process of writing a book will attest to the sacrifices that must be made both by the author and often those in his or her immediate circle of friends, family, and colleagues. The completion of this book would not have been possible without the gracious support of:

- Kim, Ryan, and Olivia. You guys are my reason for doing what I do.
- My staff at Legacy Business Cultures for kicking me out of the office and making it easy for me to "let go" of the business in order to write this book.
- John and Anita for the use of your "writer's retreat" in the sun.
- Casie Vogel for providing much-needed editorial structure, flexibility, and support.
- Michelle, Antonia, Sidney, Deb, Melanie, Michele, Paul, Fernando, Greg, Ana, Darren, Nancy and everyone else who unselfishly shared their time and expertise to help with proofreading.
- Denny Engel for welcoming me into your family and treating me as one of your own so many years ago. Even though you're no longer with us in body, the memories of your smile, laughter, kindness and intelligence seem to only get stronger with time.

I'd like to also thank all those who generously gave of their time, even on weekends, to share their stories, experiences, and perceptions about this very important topic.

Introduction

Why Focus on Respect?

E verybody is motivated by something. Likewise, there's also something that can motivate people to change. It's just a matter of figuring out what the levers are for each person. As it pertains to treating others with respect, there have historically been two important arguments that people have advocated. In recent years, additional arguments have surfaced.

According to statistics published by the Equal Employment Opportunity Commission (EEOC), U.S. corporations paid $445.8 million to settle discrimination-related violations in 2012. Frighteningly, these figures represented only reported fines paid for those cases that went to court and did not include attorney and other legal fees incurred. They also did not include money spent reaching settlements for claims that did not go to court, damage to corporate "good will," and lost workplace productivity. While hard data for these costs are not available because settlement details are often kept confidential, some estimates put them at over four times the actual amount of fines collected. It is safe to assume that U.S. businesses spent over $2 billion to settle claims of disrespectful, and typically unlawful, behavior. You don't have to major in finance to be impressed by the potential cost of disrespect, either individual or systemic.

The second reason used to advocate for greater respect at work is the case for social justice. Philosophically, I and many others believe that there are some things that are just basically right to do. One of these things is treating others with respect and dignity, no matter who they are. The problem is that not everybody goes along with this. Some people may nod their heads in agreement that respect is important and that we owe it to each other, but if it doesn't impact them personally, they're not likely to change their behavior—especially not because someone like me comes along and says it's the right thing to do.

A third reason is now emerging as a compelling motivation for focusing on respect: biology. Each of our brains is profoundly influenced by how we're treated by others. There are no smoke and mirrors here, just neurons, neurotransmitters, and electrical impulses. When we're treated with respect, our brains literally light up and perform at the highest levels at which they're capable. When we're treated with disrespect, the higher thought processes in our brains go dormant. Hijacked by our primitive survival wiring, we become diminished assets to our employers and their organizations.

Linked to this third reason is yet a fourth. When we are able to create work environments that consistently value, esteem, and nurture our employees, we increase something called employee engagement. Simply stated, engaged employees become emotionally committed to the success of their organizations and are much more likely to give their highest levels of discretionary effort when they're performing their work. In their minds, the success of their employer becomes entwined with their own personal success.

There is one final reason worth mentioning for focusing on respect: your legacy. Five or ten years in the future, the people you interact with today aren't going to remember the exact things you said and did. Whether it was during a staff meeting, at a sales conference, or on the golf course, the memories will fade. They also aren't going to remember how late you worked, what time you showed up in the morning, or your spouse's name. At least most people won't, because that's not how the human brain works.

While it's not great at remembering details, in most cases the brain does a superb job of recording our emotional experiences as we go through life. We remember people we met by how we typically felt when we were in their presence. If we were usually happy around them, we imagine they were smiling and kind to us. If we felt confident and proud, then we remember them guiding and supporting us. If we felt awkward, intimidated, or inferior around them, we re-create their demeanor and behavior accordingly. Credit goes to the brain's limbic system for this unique methodology of remembering people and events.

Whether we realize it or not, how we engage others leaves a lasting imprint. We're literally building our own legacy in their minds, one interaction at a time. Having long since forgotten the details, people will simply remember how they felt around us and then make up the rest of the story to match. When others think of us, will they smile and fondly reminisce or will they quickly "switch channels" and find a happier memory to dwell upon? An important question to ask ourselves is, how do we want to be remembered? More importantly, what are we willing to do to start responsibly building our legacy today?

PART I

The Road to Respect

CHAPTER 1 A Transformational Power

While there have been many proud moments in my career, one of the most memorable was a three-month period in 1987. I was in the second quarter of a two-term internship with the Bendix Heavy Vehicle division of AlliedSignal Corporation. I was fortunate to report to a man named Larry Taylor, who remains one of the best managers I can ever remember having. What made Larry special as a manager was that he never treated me as anything other than a fully competent associate, even though I was still a college student. His management style was to probe the outer edges of my intelligence, problem-solving skills, and creativity on a continual basis.

One particular assignment still makes me smile every time I think back to it. One day, Larry said that he had an important project for me. The company was considering an acquisition, and he wanted me to prepare a full strategic analysis of the companies being considered. More importantly, he asked that I come back to him with a recommendation once my analysis was complete. I remember feeling both excited and frightened. For a kid still in college, this was the kind of project that would require me to pull from every business discipline I had been exposed to up until that point.

The project took almost two months to complete. In the end, I presented a full analysis of three potential acquisition targets, including their financial strength, market position, reputation within

3

our industry, and range of products and services. While all three companies were attractive candidates, there was one that stood out to me as clearly being the best target. My analysis and recommendations, including multiple graphs and charts, took the form of a 60-page report with my name squarely on the cover page. I still remember walking into Larry's office, handing it to him, and proudly saying, "Here you go." At that time, it represented not only a meaningful departure from term papers and case studies, but it was also the best work I was capable of producing.

Later that afternoon, my desk phone rang, and Larry asked me to come to his office. He said, "I have reviewed your report and recommendation, and it is excellent. It's so good that I have already sent it to Dave and would like you to present it to him in person tomorrow." Dave was Larry's boss and responsible for all aftermarket strategy and marketing for our group.

This level of recognition for my work, and its implied confidence in me, was somewhat unexpected. What an impact it had. The euphoria and motivation it instilled in me lasted for years. It set the stage for me to accept the company's offer to work for it as a full-time employee once I graduated from college even though I had two offers at slightly higher starting salaries.

> As we look ahead into the next century, leaders will be those who empower others.
>
> Bill Gates, Cofounder and Chairman of Microsoft

Looking back through the 25-year lens of my experiences, it's only now that I fully appreciate the complex and powerful forces put into play that year. More than anything, Larry primed my emotional pump by treating me in a manner that made me feel smart, capable, and important. He also helped me feel like I was part of the team and see how my contributions played an integral part in the long-term strategic and financial success of the business. While he probably didn't realize it at the time, his intentional and consistent demonstration of respect for me as a person and young professional helped set in motion the productive and rewarding trajectory for the first 10 years of my professional career. Because of his communication of confidence in me, I developed a powerful emotional tie to both my boss and the company. Whether it's a project, acquisition, or purchase of equipment, either mentally or physically businesses map their return on investment (ROI). In this case, the investment was in me, and the return was the maximum engagement of my skills for the betterment of the company. What can a company do to maximize the return on investment it's made in its employees? A good starting place is to make respect an integral part of the company's corporate culture.

CHAPTER 2 Connected Through Evolution

One of the most illuminating perspectives on human interaction that I've read recently was in Daniel Goleman's book, *Primal Leadership*.[1] Goleman refers to human beings as "open loop systems." From an evolutionary perspective, our species is more connected to each other than most people realize. Over the course of millions of years, our ancestors developed highly specialized brain circuitry that constantly monitored other people when we were in their presence. In psychology, there's a concept called *theory of mind* which refers to the ability to identify mental states (beliefs, desires, intentions, perspectives, etc.) in ourselves and others, and to realize that the two states are often different. Grasping this basic difference in orientations was a remarkable and uniquely human adaptation. In a world of limited resources, it was the equivalent of developing our own personal threat detection systems.

The emotional brain responds to an event more quickly than the thinking brain.

Daniel Goleman, Author, Psychologist and Science Journalist

From an evolutionary perspective, this makes complete sense. The ability to predict accurately the peaceful or hostile intentions of new people or animals literally promoted the longevity of our species. What is fascinating about this circuitry is that it's forever in the "on" mode. What this means is that we're always monitoring other people around us, and they're doing the same. Our conclusions about the intentions of others have a profound effect on how the rest of our brain functions. Informed by inputs from our five senses, our brains perform a delicate and instinctual dance every day in the name of self-preservation.

Armed with this complex warning system, the human brain is the world's most sophisticated survival computer ever developed. Whenever our senses pick up cues that could indicate that we are or could be in the presence of danger, ancient neural pathways become activated to get us out of harm's way as quickly and effectively as possible. This is the realm of fight or flight. So powerful are these impulses that they literally commandeer the brain and order all other nonessential thinking functions to go dormant. This means that all our higher-order brain capabilities, such as problem solving, reasoning, evaluating alternatives, planning, socializing, and empathizing, are subordinated to protecting ourselves in the presence of perceived threats. This includes more than just physical threats; it also includes threats to our emotional well-being, social status, financial security, and future opportunities.

Conversely, when we interpret cues from others to mean that we are safe in their midst, our higher-level thought processes go back online, and we return to a normal level of thinking and intellectual/operational output. This "all systems safe" mode of brain function is hopefully where most of us spend the majority of our waking hours getting things done for our employers, our families, and ourselves.

From a workplace perspective, there is a mode that's more beneficial and desirable than "all systems safe." It is the mode in which we function when we perceive ourselves to be free from danger and in the presence of those who appreciate us, value what we contribute, and deem our best effort as being essential to the overall success of the group. It is also the mode in which we are constructively challenged, given opportunities and resources to be successful, and can share in the rewards of our collaboration with others. When we operate in this type of rich, stimulating, and emotionally nourishing environment, our brains are more productive than normal. They release powerful neurotransmitters that stimulate our creativity and our desire to work collaboratively; they also allow us to find deep personal satisfaction in our work. This is the *respect effect*.

The Neurology of Human Interaction

Human evolution and biology play significant roles in determining how we interact and behave around each other. Our brains are wired for speed and efficiency and powered almost exclusively by glucose, which is the form of sugar our bodies metabolize from carbohydrates. Because we have limited supplies of glucose available throughout the day, one of our natural, and often unacknowledged biases is to stay in environments that are familiar and use neural pathways that are already well-developed. When we're surrounded by people who are like us (or at least very familiar to us), we expend less glucose (energy) to understand their actions and predict their intentions. This preference for familiarity, predictability, and safety is likely one of the underlying factors that drove our ancestors to form tribes.

When we're around people for whom we have no first-hand reference points, our brains immediately try to match what we can perceive about them (visually, audibly, and through our sense of smell) to patterns that already exist. According to authors Marsh, Mendoza-Denton, and Smith:

> *Neuroscience has shown that people can identify another person's apparent race, gender, and age in a matter of milliseconds. In this blink of an eye, a complex network of stereotypes, emotional prejudices, and behavioral impulses activates.*[2]

These mental shortcuts allow us to quickly evaluate people and our relative safety around them. There is strong evidence that they also permit the brain to consume less of the body's precious supply of glucose. When we have no existing reference points for a person, event, or situation, the brain must work harder and burn considerably more energy to program new neuronal reference points and synaptic pathways. Think of it as the difference between driving down a highway versus having to build that highway in the first place. Once our "highways" are built, we are comfortable staying on them as much as possible. To a degree, this analogy helps underscore the power and persistence of stereotypes to influence our perceptions and initial interaction behaviors with others.

What Is Respect?

The word *respect* has its origins in the Latin noun *respectus,* which translates literally to: the act of looking back, and the Latin verb, *respicere,* which means to look back. Today, the actual word, as it pertains to people, has evolved to be defined by Merriam-Webster the following ways:

> *Respect: noun - 1) the act of giving particular attention: consideration, 2) high or special regard: esteem, 3) the quality of being esteemed.*
> *Respect: verb - 1a) to consider worthy of high regard: esteem, 1b) to refrain from interfering with, 2) to have reference to: concern.*

Respect is a word with enormous scope that has gradually morphed to mean different things since its first use in the fourteenth century. What makes the word so important is that, when experienced, it triggers powerful, positive emotions that not only feel good but change our behaviors. Of critical significance is that these emotional responses seem to be universal. While the actions and decisions that trigger the feeling of being respected will vary from person to person and culture to culture, the core emotion is experienced identically in all human beings. Respect *feels* the same, no matter your age, race, gender, religion, or level of intelligence or ability. Similarly, the neurological responses to being treated with respect appear to be universal. We will explore these later.

A Forward-Looking Definition

I suggest the following as a reference point for further exploring respect as a cultural component:

> *Respect is an active process of nonjudgmentally engaging people from all backgrounds. It is practiced to increase our awareness and effectiveness and demonstrated in a manner that esteems both us and those with whom we interact.*

One implication of this definition is that it doesn't permit complacency or a status quo level of social comfort. The genuine pursuit of respect requires effort, takes time, and will likely feel awkward occasionally as we push ourselves to engage people from whom we have historically kept our distance. Neurologically, the more different from us others appear, the more energy our brains have to expend to categorize and make sense of the differences. Part of this mental effort is spent creating new neural pattern circuits. Another part is spent turning down the volume of our inner voices that want to use shortcuts to process the differences.

When defining respect, the inclusion of esteem also deserves discussion. Whether or not our interactions with others have been successful in conveying respect will depend on the emotional state of others after interacting with us. If our efforts have succeeded, the desired result is for those we interact with to feel valued in some way, as colleagues, coworkers, friends, neighbors, or simply as people. When we make ourselves partially responsible for the emotional well-being of those around us, it enhances our own sense of esteem. Think of it as the "pay it forward" effect.

What this definition does *not* mean is that all our conversations with others will be pleasant and that difficult situations can't be discussed. It's quite the opposite. This definition of respect actually requires that we engage in candid conversations with individuals with whom we have problems. If employees who report to us are not performing at the required level, it is critical that we share this information with them. In order to maintain or build esteem in a person whose performance is inadequate, it is important that we separate the person from the performance. We can give candid feedback about their performance, while letting the individual know that we value him as a person and want him to succeed. Even more impactful is making it clear that our intent is to do whatever we can to help them become successful. From the perspective of the people receiving feedback, they are more willing to hear critical feedback about their performance provided they feel cared about as a person and that someone is committed to helping them meet their requirements.

Respect Is Not Tolerance

Imagine that your spouse, partner, or significant other came home from work one Friday afternoon and, with a smile on his or her, enthusiastically declared that he loved his job because his boss and coworkers *tolerated* him. We would probably look at him as if he had a screw loose because the feeling of being tolerated and his expression of joy didn't match! Most people don't associate the feeling of being tolerated with overt happiness, smiles, and energy. That's not to say that tolerance is bad; it's simply a mediocre standard given the alternatives. Think of it as receiving a rating of "average" on your performance review. It's not an unsatisfactory, but it doesn't put your workplace performance at a level that can lead to a personal and/or monetary reward.

Whenever we interact with others, either at work or in our private lives, there is a broad range of possible behaviors that we can demonstrate (see Figure 2.1). Tolerating others is a neutral position. It is not positive or negative in its impact and requires little energy to initiate and sustain. This is why people typically perceive themselves as being tolerant. When surveyed, most people indicate that they are more tolerant than those around them (the "better than

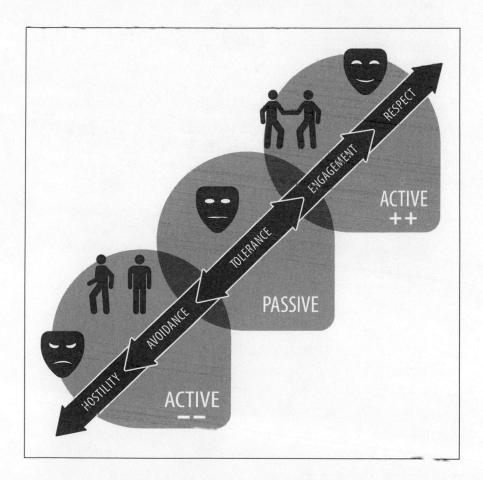

Figure 2.1   The road to respect

average" effect). We would find it difficult to refute these internal and usually unspoken, beliefs because the demonstration of tolerance has few behaviors or actions associated with it. The possible exception is when we are around others who we perceive to be annoying; then tolerance requires effort.

The Island of Misfit Toys

If you've ever eaten at a Hard Rock Cafe, one of the first things that made an impression on you was the outstanding collection of rock and roll memorabilia gracing the walls. The next thing you noticed is the equally memorable collection of stage-ready staffers employed by Hard Rock to provide you with a remarkable dining experience. Tattoos, body piercings, Mohawks or spiked hair in all colors with clothes to match can create an almost uneasy feeling for first-time Hard Rock patrons. My first visit in 2009 (Baltimore, Maryland) was this way. That is, until I was greeted with a huge smile, amazingly friendly attitude, and a simple welcome, "Hi, my name is Gordon, and I'll be your server today. Have you ever eaten at a Hard Rock before?" As I sat in our booth with my wife and young kids, I cautiously said, "No, this is our first time." Gordon beamed. "Cool! You're going to love it here. By the way, only my parents call me Gordon. You can call me Sly!" With that, my apprehensions vanished.

According to Jim Knight, Sr., director of training and development for Hard Rock International, the previously described and authentic greeting is what sets the tone for an amazing guest experience. It's also part of the Hard Rock's unique formula for success in the restaurant industry that each year sees a higher-than-average failure rate for new entrants. It is part of the same formula that propelled the company to legendary patron status and solid financial performance since Americans Peter Morton and Isaac Tigrett opened the first restaurant in London, England in 1971.

The Hard Rock guest experience starts with the hiring process for its distinctive staff. Knight has a direct hand in training the majority of management personnel within the organization. "We're kind of like the Island of Misfit Toys from the television Christmas special," he grinned during a recent interview in Orlando, Florida. "We look to hire employees who, because of their individuality, might not fit in with more traditional restaurants."

He went on to say, "There's something special about the chemistry between our staffers because they're all kind of outsiders in some way or another. The Hard Rock guest experience is a direct result of this *'we're all freaks'* chemistry. It kind of results in a flavor of teamwork and commitment that, quite honestly, I've never seen matched in other hospitality-related organizations."

The spike-haired and energetic Knight modestly tried to minimize his own influence. When pressed, he acknowledged his hands-on style of training and development content for Hard Rock managers. The element that appears to be most important is an emphasis on creating a "rock star" experience for customers and employees. This approach is obviously a winner because the chain boasts patron evaluations that are best-in-class, and a staff turnover that is half the industry average. To an outsider looking in, the connection seems obvious.

Knight has been part of the Hard Rock team for over 20 years. What keeps him there? It's more than the Rolex watch—each employee, no matter what their position, gets one after 10 years. It's more than the ability to travel the world and knowing he's personally making a difference. Reflecting on the company's underlying approach, *Do well by doing well*, he said, "This place is kind of in my DNA. I love what I do, love the people I do it with and love the guests we all do it for." On the wall directly behind Knight's head is one of the several short sayings for which the Hard Rock Cafe is so famous:—*Love all—Serve all.*

Once we move away from the relatively passive mode of simply tolerating others, we start exerting energy, typically mental and occasionally physical. We start *behaving* around others in relation to our perceptions of what their presence signifies. Those behaviors are predicated on our stored knowledge, including the stereotypes that we have about them or people like them. Here's where our evolutionary instincts enter into the equation. Our first genetically imprinted directive is to remain safe. People feel safest when they are around others who are like them. The problem is that given the vast range of dissimilarities among people, we perceive most people as different from us. A colleague suggested to me years ago that many of us unintentionally alienate ourselves from others merely by our self-perceived sense of "terminal uniqueness."

When we perceive that we are interacting with unfamiliar people who have unknown or suspect motives, the natural emotion that surfaces is suspicion (or, minimally, caution). The behavioral manifestation of suspicion is avoidance. The same response can be expected when we are in the presence of people for whom we have stereotyped information that suggests unpredictable or hostile intentions. Over the course of our evolution, this "play it safe" response kept our ancestors out of harm's way and increased our chances of long-term survival. In situations in which the presence of unfamiliar people suggests impending conflict or danger, our level of physical and mental energy usage goes up beyond avoidance. We prepare ourselves to initiate or protect ourselves from hostility.

Life today is very different from the world in which our prehistoric ancestors fought for survival. While there are occasional situations in which we perceive physical danger, potentially dangerous people are more likely to threaten us with psychological, emotional, or social harm. That's why the term *hostility* needs to be defined broadly:

Hostile behavior is an intentional activity that harms another person in any way, including physically, emotionally, socially, financially, professionally, or by reputation. Hostility can also be demonstrated by behaviors that intentionally impede others in meeting their predetermined goals.

For those employed in workplaces where hostile behaviors are openly tolerated or even encouraged, there is little doubt to the damage inflicted on productivity. Energy spent perpetrating or deflecting hostility is energy that can't be spent doing the work individuals were hired to do.

Hostile behaviors are at the polar opposite end of the spectrum from behaviors associated with respect. The question is what will send our behavior in a different direction, away from avoidance and hostility and toward *engagement*. The answer is remarkably simple. While initially not easy, selectively rewiring our brains to respond to differences with *curiosity* instead of suspicion is the most direct path. When practiced, cultivating an attitude of curiosity about the differences between ourselves and others leads to an entirely different set of behaviors and actions. When we're curious about something or someone, rather than avoiding them, we should engage them to explore the differences. It is this active demonstration of curiosity that leads us to explore the unique individuality that differentiates us from others. It is also the path that leads us to discover similarities that may not be visible on the surface and ultimately, to respect.

The benefits of curiosity notwithstanding, it would be naïve to think that there was never a place for suspicion in our world. Not every situation or person is safe to be around. To walk alone at night in a part of town that has a statistically higher incidence of physical crime would be foolhardy. Similarly, letting your guard down around a person who treated you with hostility in the past would be unwise. No species would survive if it completely ignored known threats to its safety and well-being.

An attitude of curiosity starts with the intention to exit our familiar orbit and subordinate our more primal fear of the unknown.

But there has to be a value proposition for doing so; a future benefit linked to learning more about others or we won't exert the effort required to refocus our attention. A degree of mindfulness is also helpful; being observant when our minds initially tell us to be careful and being able to push back gently with reason and ask ourselves, "What is the danger?"

As we learn to turn down the volume of our own "noise," we become more aware of stories about other people and their imagined intentions. This is part of our explanatory style, our ability to explain to ourselves why we experience a particular event, either positive or negative. Uncovering and owning our current stories, even the unpleasant ones, allow us to begin to test them through reason and a fresh outlook. Do our apprehensions and suspicions make sense logically, or are they simply leftover artifacts from inherited stereotypes and past experiences that are too old to be relied upon accurately to predict the future?

> If you have some respect for people as they are, you can be more effective in helping them to become better than they are.
>
> John W. Gardner, Educator, Public Official and Political Reformer

While more tangible benefits typically come later, curiosity leads to a process of discovery that is intrinsically enjoyable and valuable. When we mutually make the time to get to know others at levels beyond what the senses can detect, there is a covalidation that takes place for all parties. Some cultures have a specific vocabulary to describe this process. In Bantu (African), it's sometimes referred to as *Ubuntu* (pronounced oo-BUUN-too), "I am what I am because of who we all are." *Namaste* (pronounced NAH-məs-tay) from India translates to, "The spirit in me respects the spirit in you." When we acknowledge and validate each other, we become connected and a part of something bigger. This discovery process, taking varying degrees of effort, leads us to the doorstep of respect.

Making a Difference with Mutual Respect

In the summer of 2010, Medical Mutual of Ohio launched Mutual Respect, an initiative that would build on the company's already strong employee satisfaction ratings and turn them into an active force to improve areas including customer service, employee commitment, and trust. According to Tom Greene, vice president of human resources in a personal interview with Legacy Business Cultures staffers, "The goal of any program of this type should be to create an environment that, over time, will continue to foster retention, improve employee continuity, and make for a better customer experience. All of those characteristics help differentiate Medical Mutual in the marketplace."

Support for the idea came straight from the top. The board of directors of Medical Mutual recognized that their people were their company's greatest competitive advantage. Patty Hartmann, manager of corporate learning and development, noted that both the board and senior leadership wanted to leverage the company's diversity, not as a passive way to recognize people's differences, but to use them actively to make Medical Mutual stronger. "We knew we had a culture that understood diversity and supported differences," said Hartmann in a personal interview. "But we wanted to turn that into a competitive asset that helped us succeed in the market. It's the next step in continuing to build an inclusive culture."

Medical Mutual officially launched Mutual Respect by first surveying all 2,700 of its employees in Ohio, Indiana, South Carolina, and Georgia to establish internal benchmark data on perceptions of respectfulness in the culture. In a personal interview, Sandy Opacich, director of

continued

human resources stated, "We have been doing employee satisfaction surveys for several years, but with Legacy on board, we were able to interweave questions developed specifically to ascertain the level of respect within." The initial survey response rate was 70 percent, which was substantial. The results showed that, while Medical Mutual was already perceived as a respectful work environment, there was room for improvement in some key areas.

Acting on data and insights gained from the survey process, Medical Mutual quickly followed up with a customized training curriculum designed to position respect as a platform for better understanding of the broader concept of diversity and how to leverage it for culture change. Medical Mutual's training partner was quick to point out that an authentic culture of respect goes beyond the traditional (diversity) focus on awareness of differences. While this may be a good starting point, authentic respect requires the active commitment of all managers and employees to treat one another in ways that build esteem and communicate value.

Initially, a half-day workshop was delivered to all leaders and managers, including the chief executive officer. Following the management workshops, each manager was required to work with his or her team members to facilitate the creation of a code of cooperation. These "living guidelines" typically included 8–12 behaviorally specific statements detailing how employees who work together agreed to engage with and treat each other. What sets Mutual Respect apart from past diversity efforts, according to Medical Mutual's Tom Greene, is that, The results of the survey and the manager-level training include a clear link to organization-wide efforts to foster a culture of respect."

With management already having completed the program, Medical Mutual is now offering over 30 sessions of the Mutual Respect workshop to all employees on a voluntary basis. Their business partner has certified internal staff members to facilitate the workshop, and Hartmann says it has been very well attended. "So far, all sessions have been full, most with waiting lists," she says. "We re-surveyed our employees in third-quarter 2011 and, judging by the results, we do see a definite connection between perceptions of respect and other metrics like retention, which have a measurable impact on our company."

CHAPTER 3 Our Brains on Respect

Biology and Emotions

In order to understand the potential that respect has for unleashing the best in an organization, we first have to recognize what it does at the individual level. There are all sorts of behaviors—many that vary from culture to culture and even from person to person—that may trigger the emotional feeling of respect in the recipient. Here are just a few:

- Offering a verbal compliment
- Making direct eye contact
- Supporting their work and objectives
- Addressing them by their first name
- Showing concern for their health and well-being
- Sharing your limited resources
- Making a personal sacrifice for them
- Giving them public recognition
- Seeking their opinion on an important matter
- Offering assistance to help them succeed
- Showing an interest in their work
- Giving them your undivided attention
- Referring or recommending them to others

- Defending them in front of others
- Including them in an important discussion
- Asking them for assistance
- Referring to their opinion and expertise
- Showing an interest in their family
- Validating their opinions and ideas
- Being completely candid
- Empathizing with a setback or loss

What's interesting about these behaviors and their supporting entourage of verbal and nonverbal cues is that they all have the potential to evoke strong, positive emotion. More specifically, they trigger the release of powerful and pleasurable chemicals in our brains that we interpret as positive emotions. Dr. Ellen Weber, director, MITA Brain Based Center, was recently quoted in *HR Magazine*:

> *Social fairness and respect help employees learn. When we show interest in others, support them and praise them genuinely, we "squirt" a chemical mix of serotonin and oxytocin into their brains. These neurotransmitters encourage trust, open others' minds to our ideas, and create desire to get to know us better and to help with whatever we need done.*[1]

Over the years, I've queried literally thousands of participants on the emotions that surface when they are treated with respect. Here is just a small sampling of their responses:

- Happy
- Energized
- Intelligent
- Committed
- Vital
- Needed
- Part of the group
- Motivated
- Inspired to work even harder
- Honored
- Trusted
- Important

- Safe
- Engaged
- Accepted

- Proud
- Validated
- Valued

Positive Emotions Drive Productivity

On the surface, this feel-good list of emotions looks nice. But does it make a difference in the quality and quantity of work people do? To answer this question, imagine that when you leave your home to go to work each day, you take an invisible backpack that contains all your emotions. When you arrive at work, your backpack probably contains emotions that were generated by your commute. Rather than leaving this backpack in your locker or desk, you carry it with you throughout the day. Every time you interact with someone, the contents of the backpack change to reflect the emotional quality of your interaction.

Do these emotions cause a change? When asked, the vast majority of respondents answered in the affirmative. The universal response I have received on five continents can be summarized this way: *In the presence of these emotions, we are likely to be doing the very best work we are capable of for our organizations.* That level of effort can translate into significant organizational advantages.

Higher job satisfaction and employee engagement
When people are consistently treated with respect by colleagues and coworkers, they enjoy being at work and are more likely to become emotionally committed to the success of their organization. Research conducted by the Gallup Organization, among others, has linked elevated levels of employee engagement to significantly higher levels of productivity and profitability when compared to businesses in the same industry that have lower levels of engagement.[2]

Employee engagement is different from employee satisfaction and is a better indicator of the emotional connection employees have to their organizations. Dr. Paul Marciano made the following observation: "Indeed, engagement is all about commitment; the word comes from the old French (en + gage) meaning 'to pledge oneself'." Although not quite so life altering, the concept of employee engagement is also about the extent to which one is committed, dedicated, and loyal to one's organization, supervisor, work, and colleagues. When you're truly committed, motivation becomes a lot less relevant—you're in it for the long haul.[3]

Improved physical and emotional health of associates

Employees who can count on and anticipate respectful interactions at work are typically beneficiaries of better physical health. Dr. Michael Roizen from the Cleveland Clinic suggests that, with very few exceptions, the quality of our relationships with others is an even greater predictor of our physical health than our personal lifestyles and habits.[4]

Improved ability to attract, develop, and retain talented employees

When workplaces have a reputation for being consistently respectful, they also tend to be more fun, energetic, and collaborative. These are the qualities that make businesses attractive to both potential and current employees. Innovative companies are finding that they need to spend less money and time searching for new employees because their own "cultural brand" sells itself. Potential employees seek out these businesses for employment opportunities, and current employees become active in recruiting new employees. Engaged, happy, and productive employees tend to want to surround themselves with other people like themselves.

Improved information flow and organizational learning

You don't have to pry information loose from people in respectful workplaces. Freely sharing information important to the business is commonplace. Competitor and customer updates come in from the field and are quickly shared with other parts of the organization. Opinions, suggestions, and observations about strategy are shared without reservation. Problems and setbacks are openly discussed and collaboratively resolved.

Improved customer satisfaction

Smiles are contagious, even over the phone. Employees who are consistently treated with respect tend to maintain happier, friendlier dispositions. They are prone to making themselves emotionally available and empathetic to the needs of their customers and clients. Customers, including patients, who feel that their service providers genuinely care about trying to help them, are more likely to remain customers. They also frequently share their positive views with others.

Higher organizational productivity, profitability, and resilience

One of the biggest benefits we gain from creating respectful workplaces is that we increase our bandwidth or ability to successfully engage in more than one thing at a time. More energy and commitment are available for creativity, innovation, and problem solving when employees and managers are emotionally healthy. We bring our best selves to work and take great pride in utilizing our talents for the betterment of the company. A good word to describe this type of work environment is authentic. When we create emotionally safe environments that allow all employees to be authentic, to comfortably bring their entire selves to work, we free up incredible energy that might otherwise be used to protect or defend.

Even in times of change, employees who work in respectful workplaces find it easier to work collaboratively to accomplish what needs to be done. This is the result of the level of trust that exists between people. When individuals know that the people they work with "have their backs" and can be trusted to support them, they focus more of their energies on managing changes in the environment instead of on their relationships.

Respect—The Invisible Force Behind Zappos

In a small, downtown Las Vegas coffee shop, Tony Hsieh, founder of online super-retailer Zappos, thoughtfully shared his opinion on the power of respect. As captured in his best selling book, *Delivering Happiness* (Writers Of The Round Table Press, 2012), he identified Zappos' 10 Core Values as the foundation for the company's success. Curiously, not one of the values explicitly mentions the word *respect*. How could Zappos create a path to profits, passion, and purpose without an emphasis on respect? "You can't," answered Hsieh.

As a company, Zappos understands exactly how important culture is to both the employees and the long-term success of the business. Hsieh explained, "Culture is to a company as communities are to a city." Indeed, his hobby is to study the great cities of the world and analyze their growth patterns. He continued, "When a city doubles in size, the culture doesn't die; it evolves." When Zappos moved from San Francisco to Las Vegas in 2003, the company had only 60 employees. Today, the number exceeds 1,300. The core cultural elements that propelled its start-up years ago are still the ones that help it consistently rank as one of the best places to work by Forbes. Zappos is on the move again, and in 2013 it will take over the old City Hall building in downtown Las Vegas. Success will surely follow.

Every year, Zappos asks its employees to e-mail their responses to a single question: "What does the Zappos culture mean to you?" The unedited responses are then combined and published in the *Zappos*

Culture Book. Like an annual rite of passage, this document has become a cornerstone for helping current employees communicate and perpetuate the culture that has made the company so successful. Even customers and vendors can weigh in. One recently wrote, "The Zappos culture is all about respect. Respect for their employees, vendors, and most importantly, customers." In some cases, employees share deeply personal stories. One entry in the 2011 edition read, "Zappos has changed my life. Every day, I am around people who respect each other and are not afraid to be themselves." When asked how entries such as these made him feel, Hsieh said, "I guess if they didn't say those things, I would be sad."

With sales topping $1 billion in 2009, and a recent acquisition by Amazon promising more of the same in the future, Zappos has continued to evolve. And just like the cities Hsieh has studied, growth means change. The company was recently split into 10 separate business units, each still committed to the core values required for "delivering happiness." Curiously, this includes helping other organizations find their own path to profits, passion, and purpose. "Respect is, in a way, the foundation for our culture, and now we intentionally share that with others." Hsieh continued, "Without respect in our workplace, Zappos simply would not be here today."

The final question for Hsieh had to do with how he and other leaders within Zappos handle any complaints of disrespect in their workplace. He quickly replied, "If it cannot be successfully handled within the workgroup, we fire them." Zero tolerance for disrespect is one of the ways that respect has become an ingrained part of the Zappos culture—without it ever being mentioned by name.

CHAPTER 4 # The Destructive Power of Disrespect

J ust as respect triggers a complex release of neurotransmitters that bring about certain emotions, disrespect does the same. The results, however, are considerably different.

My personal experience with disrespect involves a former strategic partner. Working with a long-term client for several months, I created an opening for one of our partners to provide services through our company. The effort culminated in our making an on-site sales call at the client's headquarters in Virginia. The call was spectacularly successful, and we ended up winning a contract worth almost $250,000. Even though most of that would go to our partner, I was thrilled with the outcome because my client was happy. More importantly, the path was set for future collaboration.

Unfortunately, what started out as a successful venture soon fell apart. Shortly after the sales call, "Phil," the vice president of sales for our partner, called me and laid into me with a display of foul language, name-calling, and accusations that left me speechless. Evidently, I took too much of the lead in the call for his liking. I had positioned myself into the subsequent client management activities more than he wanted, even though it was my customer. For good measure, he finished his assault by criticizing my personal sales skills as not being aggressive enough in promoting my own services.

> When once the forms of civility are violated, there remains little hope of return to kindness or decency.
>
> Samuel Johnson, English Poet, Critic and Writer

About 30 seconds into the call, I distinctly remember having an almost out-of-body experience, wondering if the conversation was really taking place. No warning, no gradual escalation of emotion. Just an oral ambush and with no place for me to hide. My brain locked down, and I was powerless. Was this an anomaly or was this Phil's typical behavior? Was he under stress and this was how he normally responded when things didn't go his way? It didn't matter at that point. While Phil was relatively new in his position, I had worked with his company's founders for several years. The entire relationship was compromised in that 90-second conversation. We eventually won the contract, but that was the last time I ever introduced that partner to one of my clients. I intentionally hired an employee shortly after that incident that had the skill set necessary to bring that company's core service offering in-house. It is now a major profit center for my business.

This example demonstrates how quickly disrespect can destroy something that took years to build. In this case, the primary casualty was trust. While Phil may have had some valid points, whatever those were and my willingness to consider them were lost because of the way his message was delivered. His attacking style put me immediately on the defensive and literally short-circuited the parts of my brain that are responsible for reflection and evaluation. It is important to note that I didn't just lose trust in Phil. I also lost trust in those who hired him and never did business with them again.

Widespread Damage

In addition to my story, I have had workshop participants from all levels within their companies share stories about having been treated with disrespect. Shop floor workers, customer service associates, front-line supervisors, and senior leaders all had stories about being treated poorly. Some of the incidents happened years ago. The greater the degree of perceived disrespect, the more quickly and vividly the incidents were recalled. Some of the behavior mentioned included:

- Was lied to
- Was excluded from important meeting
- Had his idea laughed at publicly
- Was intentionally excluded from social activities
- Was subjected to gender stereotyping
- Was propositioned even though married
- Was told he was not promotable because of the college he attended
- Was told he dressed funny
- Was expected to reply to routine text messages late at night
- Had an interviewee interrupt the interview to respond to a text
- Was referred to by an ethnic slur
- Was the subject of gossip
- Manager took credit for her idea
- Was routinely interrupted and talked over
- Was verbally taunted
- Was subjected to proselytizing
- Had her physical attributes discussed publicly
- Had his confidential comments made public
- Had her boss skip an important meeting to go golfing
- Had boss interrupt annual performance review to call his stock broker

- Was subjected to sexual innuendo
- Was cursed and yelled at
- Was blamed for someone else's error
- Was spoken to in a condescending manner
- Was held to a different standard than peers
- Was told he was too old to be promoted
- Was subjected to eye rolls, sighs, and other disrespectful nonverbal signals
- Was told to "get a clue" by her boss
- Was told to shut up by his supervisor in front of his peers

What's interesting about these disrespectful behaviors is that the damage they caused often wasn't restricted to the direct recipient. When we observe someone treating another person disrespectfully, we make a note of it. It is part of our self-preservation wiring. The offending individual wasn't treating us poorly, but it could be our turn in the future. When we see the capacity for the disrespectful behavior in another person, we take note and are likely to keep that individual at arm's length so that we don't become the next victim. The greater the authority a person has in an organization, the more damage he or she can do. A senior leader who is permitted to treat underlings with routine disrespect because it is "his style" can cause tremendous damage to trust and morale within the organization. The reason these behaviors are so damaging is that the negative emotions that result have the potential to undermine both individual and group productivity.

The damage starts with a chemical release of two potent hormones—adrenaline and cortisol. Both molecules occur naturally in the body and, in small doses, play an important role in keeping us safe. The problem is that our brains don't distinguish between physical and emotional safety. The electrochemical warning systems that responded when our prehistoric ancestors were attacked by a saber tooth tiger or a predatory tribe are the same ones that are activated to protect us from an attacking dog, a swerving car, or an assailant with a gun. Our brain also responds similarly to verbal attacks, taunting, being publicly embarrassed, and receiving threatening e-mail messages. The release of cortisol and adrenaline causes the brain to focus exclusively on self-protection. In this mode, the brain shuts down a region called the prefrontal cortex that is responsible for coordinating our executive functions such as reasoning, maintaining attention, managing our impulses, evaluating alternatives, and solving problems.

When we treat people in the workplace in ways they perceive to be disrespectful, we deactivate the parts of their brains that are capable of performing the tasks they were hired to complete. We temporarily take them offline as human assets of the business. Depending on how severe the response is, it may take up to four hours for the cortisol levels to return to normal. Even then, the damage isn't over. Every time the individual replays the mental tape of the occurrence, the same chemical response is initiated by the brain. The purpose of this response is as basic as it is unstoppable: to reinforce the brain's memory of the danger and protect the individual from a similar kind of attack in the future.

Here is a sample of the many emotions that individuals have reported feeling when they were treated with disrespect and their protection circuits were activated:

- Attacked
- Sabotaged
- Inadequate
- Trapped
- Humiliated
- Unmotivated
- Fearful
- Angry
- Embarrassed
- Incompetent
- Depressed
- Insecure
- Disengaged
- Unimportant
- Confused
- Frustrated
- Hopeless
- Spiteful
- Excluded
- Paralyzed
- Defensive

How do these emotions affect the quality of our work, both individually and as a group? Let's return to the backpack analogy. Imagine going to work. By midday your backpack contains a few of the emotions listed above, and you're now carrying them wherever you go. What would be the quality of your work? What would your motivation be to do your best work? When I ask this of workshop participants, I go to great lengths to make sure that it is not viewed as a rhetorical question. After a few awkward moments of silence, someone finally speaks up and typically says, "We're not doing any work. We're just going through the motions." Even if we wanted to, our brains are physically incapable of doing their best work because they are spending a great portion of their available energy in protection mode.

When people ask me what types of organizations employ our company, I like to answer that there are two kinds. The first kind is made up of companies proactively planning and working to create respectful workplaces so that they are able to get the maximum contribution from each employee. The second kind is make up of organizations for whom the proverbial, "Horse has already gotten out of the barn."

Disrespectful Behavior and Productivity Challenges

A pattern of disrespectful behaviors causes damage and productivity-related challenges take place, such as those discussed below.

Low Employee Engagement Levels
When employees are not engaged, they are less likely to give discretionary effort on behalf of their employer. Their work performance becomes a simple monetary transaction in which they generate

whatever is perceived to be the lowest level of effort required to collect their paycheck.

Higher Rates of Stress-Related Illnesses Within Employee and Leadership Ranks

One of the more intriguing medical research discoveries in recent
years is the connection between stress hormones and cardiovascular disease. Employees in disrespectful workplaces are more likely
to show elevated levels of adrenaline and cortisol. While some levels of these compounds are necessary to keep us safe, long-term,
continual exposure can result in blood vessel lesions that eventually scar over and attract plaque. Over time, this significantly
raises the susceptibility to cardiovascular disease. This phenomenon occurs with both humans and other primate species. It doesn't
take a tremendous leap in logic to hypothesize that disrespectful
workplaces may actually end up causing their owners and workers
higher healthcare costs.

One particularly damaging demonstration of hostility is a form of
bullying that occurs when certain peers are intentionally excluded
from group-related activities. Often this behavior starts with either
work-related or social activities and then extend to the others over
time. According to a recent study highlighted in the *Journal of
Management*:

> *Workplace ostracism, an adult form of bullying, is
> often described as an individual's belief that they are
> ignored or excluded by superiors or colleagues in the
> workplace. A 2005 survey of 262 full-time employees
> found that over a five-year period, 66% of respondents
> felt they were systematically ignored by colleagues,
> and 29% reported that other people intentionally left
> the area when they entered. Previous studies have
> shown that ostracism is an interpersonal stressor that*

can lead to psychological distress. Workplace distress is strongly linked to life distress, employee turnover and poor physical health.[1]

Higher Levels of Absenteeism

When employees perceive that they are treated poorly by their peers and supervisors, they are more likely to call in sick when they are only marginally ill. We've all had those days when we think to ourselves, "I don't feel that well. Should I go to work or not?" Those who work in disrespectful work environments are less likely to go to work.

Higher Rates of Workplace Accidents

A trusted colleague of mine was formerly the director of safety for a large petroleum and chemical company. He shared with me that there was a definite connection between accidents and workplace culture. When people are treated disrespectfully, they often end up working with head and hands in different places. Quite literally, they perform their jobs without fully paying attention to what they're doing because they may be processing how to protect themselves from disrespectful treatment.

Above Industry Average Employee Turnover Rates

Disrespectful workplaces are at risk for losing key talent. When employees leave an organization on their own, they are often the employees with the most skills and potential. The reason for this is simple: they are the ones who are desired by other companies and, therefore, have more employment options. Based on years of conversations with human resource professionals, in disrespectful work environments, it is clear that there is little intrinsic motivation for these employees to stay when they can likely make the same amount of money working for a company where employees are treated better.

In 2002, Captain D. Michael Abrashoff published his *New York Times* best seller, *It's Your Ship – Management Techniques from the Best Damn Ship in the Navy.* In this book he described the results of an internal study by the U.S. Armed Forces to determine why so many service men and women were not reenlisting after their original tours of duty. He wrote:

> *Pondering all of this in the context of my post as the new captain of USS Benfold, I read some exit surveys, interviews conducted by the military to find out why people are leaving. I assumed that low pay would be the first, but in fact, it was fifth. The top reason was not being treated with respect or dignity; second was being prevented from making an impact on the organization; third, not being listened to; and forth, not being rewarded with more responsibility. Talk about an eye-opener.[2]*

Poor Communication Patterns and Practices

While not a technical description, communication patterns within organizations that tolerate disrespectful behavior can become constipated. Information gets plugged up and frequently is not shared as quickly and widely as it should be. The rationale is that in the presence of the negative emotions mentioned previously, people's motivation for how and what they communicate with others becomes skewed. Rather than sharing thoughts, opinions, and data to make sure everyone has the best information, the process becomes more calculated. People selectively share, or withhold information based on what they perceive will make them look good, create an advantage over others, or keep them out of trouble.

Lower Client Satisfaction and Higher Customer Turnover

Any organization that tolerates disrespectful behaviors involving customer interaction faces the risk of alienating its client base. This is true whether the industry is manufacturing, healthcare, insurance, or retail. People generally do a poor job of isolating emotions. If an employee feels she has been treated with disrespect by a coworker or supervisor, it is likely to impact her interactions with people who have no connection to the disrespectful behaviors. It will show up as complaining, a lack of patience, or possibly a general unwillingness to give the extra effort required to solve a problem. In certain industries, such as healthcare, this may even affect critical outcomes.

Lower Employee Productivity

While disrespect comes in many forms, it almost always damages performance. This is true at the individual level and often migrates to the group level. The primary reason is that it takes energy to respond and protect ourselves from disrespectful behaviors. Every time our brain has to divert its attention and energy to manage disrespectful elements within our environment, it represents a lost opportunity for the organization. The brain taps its store of glucose to protect itself from danger rather than apply itself to problem solving.

The disrespect doesn't have to be overt or intentional. A colleague once shared his perspective of what it was like to be gay in an organization that did not openly have a policy of inclusion for the lesbian, gay, bisexual and transgender (LGBT) members of its workforce. What this meant for him was that every day that he came to work, he had to spend a significant part of his energy simply trying to maintain the illusion that he was not gay. When people talked about what they did with their families over the weekend, he would either intentionally avoid participation in these conversations or use very guarded language that would not give away the fact that he was gay. If pressed for details, he would sometimes make things up just so he would appear to fit in with those who were straight. He had to expend additional energy making sure that what he shared on that day didn't contradict anything he might have said previously. It was an exhausting way to go through each day for five years. Think of the energy lost that could have been spent productively working.

Poor Ability to Respond to Changes in a Competitive Environment

As previously noted, the human brain only has so much energy to spend each day. Every molecule of glucose our brains have to spend protecting and defending ourselves in disrespectful environments represents energy that can't be spent on value-creating work. This includes monitoring and planning how to stay ahead of our competition, thinking about how to integrate new technology, and making sure that our customers are satisfied and thrilled to have their needs taken care. Disrespect simply becomes a distraction and energy drain on the entire organization.

What Happens When the Leader Is the Problem?

One of the greatest challenges in working with client organizations is that senior leaders and top managers often are blind to their personal role in the dysfunctional symptoms that they hire companies like mine to help resolve. In 2011, our company was retained to help with the training and development of the midlevel managers for a 400-plus person manufacturing department in a well-known consumer products company. As part of our effort, we implemented a 360-degree feedback process for everyone who was in a leadership role within the group. The purpose was to help the leaders better understand the perceptions that were driving employee attitudes within their department. It was very successful—with one exception.

The most senior member of the team, the vice president of manufacturing, did not complete the 360-degree process. At first, this was attributed to a heavy task load and a busy travel schedule. Upon further investigation and multiple second chances to participate, a different reality became apparent. This individual intentionally chose not to participate. When questioned directly, he hemmed and hawed and came up with multiple reasons why it wasn't as important for him to complete the process as it was for his staff. In hindsight, I think he may

continued

actually have believed some of his own excuses, but to an outsider, and more importantly to his own staff, it was apparent that he simply was not willing to make himself open to feedback. Sadly, comments and insights gleaned from others in the organization squarely pointed to this key player as the source of much conflict, animosity, and confusion both within and outside his group. His disrespectful behaviors included publicly criticizing those who reported directly to him and talking behind the backs of those at his own level earning him the reputation of being a back stabber.

As often happens, this vice president resigned "to pursue new opportunities" with another organization. Miraculously, not only did the morale improve within the group, but so did the group's performance and stature within the company. While this was an obvious case of addition by subtraction for both the department and the organization, I couldn't help wondering where this individual landed next and what damage he might be causing. I wonder what would have happened if he had made himself open to feedback and been willing to do the hard work required to address some of his shortcomings

CHAPTER 5 Why We Treat Each Other Poorly

Abasic question to ask at this point is why do people treat each other with disrespect? Is it based in selfishness? Does it come from our disregard for the well-being of others? Does it come from ignorance? Or could it possibly come from low self-esteem? It may be some or all of these reasons depending on the situation. One point is clear: the path toward disrespect is far easier and more convenient than the path toward respect. It takes very little to justify on the front end and can usually be rationalized after the fact by selectively tying it to the less-than-perfect behavior of others.

Psychopaths Among Us

Based on a scale created by psychologist Robert Hare, anywhere from 1–2 percent of the general population could be categorized as psychopathic. By definition, this means that they demonstrate a pervasive pattern of showing disregard for, and violating the rights of, others. Because the origins of psychopathic tendencies may be biological in nature and genetically predisposed, there may not be a lot that others can do to change or influence the behavior of psychopaths. It is crucial that individuals who fit this profile not be promoted to senior levels of leadership. As history has shown, psychopaths can be extremely successful in pursuing their goals. They also leave a wake of human destruction behind them that ends up causing severe and sometimes permanent damage to their organizations. Some of the personalities involved with the colossal implosion of Enron make this abundantly clear.

Neuroscientists estimate that a similar 1 to 2 percent of people are physiologically immune to the effects of the oxytocin molecule. This naturally occurring compound is produced by most mammals and is credited with creating emotional bonds between people. The release of oxytocin can be triggered in mothers by nursing infants, by intimate contact between couples, or simply by hugs, warm smiles, and friendly interactions. Multiple studies have shown that the presence of oxytocin increases the degree of trust that people have in those with whom they are interacting. In his extraordinarily popular TED (Technology, Entertainment and Design) Conference video (available on YouTube), University of Santa Clara author and researcher Dr. Paul Zak famously refers to the small percentage of people immune to the effects of oxytocin by a nontechnical designation. He said, "We called them bastards."

This category of individuals, as damaging as they can be, is eclipsed by the much broader population of people with other forms of psychological illness. According the National Institute of Mental Health (NIMH), an estimated 26 percent of adults suffers from a clinically diagnosable mental disorder in any given year, with over 6 percent suffering from serious mental illness. When you consider that forms of mental illness may include mood and anxiety disorders, panic and posttraumatic stress disorders, and social phobia and autism spectrum disorders, it's probably safe to suspect that many behaviors viewed by recipients as disrespectful (i.e., avoidance, micromanaging, aloofness, demonstrations of anger or frustration, etc.) are the result of personal mental health challenges.

Albeit a bit extreme, one example of how mental illness can lead directly to antisocial behavior was shared with me by "Gary," another small business owner, earlier this past year. He had a young extern named "Sarah" working for him in a part-time public relations capacity. Although he knew up front that Sarah suffered from a severe social shyness disorder (for which she was taking medication), he decided to give her an opportunity to show what she could do. Although shyness would seemingly be a detriment to a PR role, she was bright, a good communicator, and had demonstrated a strong work ethic with past work assignments.

With the exception of a few questionable behaviors that he attributed to generational differences (involving appropriate communications on social media), Sarah did a decent job. She showed up on time for work, completed her assignments in a timely fashion, and had a generally pleasant personality. At the same time, she struggled with her interactions with other employees and with being a self-starter. Because she was so shy, she frequently kept to herself in her office and rarely initiated conversations with other associates. Similarly, when she was done with tasks, she would sit and wait to be told what to do next rather than actively seeking out new ways to contribute. After five months, Sarah's overall performance was evaluated to be okay, but not ideal for a full-time position. Her assignment came to an end with an extensive performance review, a sincere thank you, and an offer to use Gary as a future reference. All seemed to be good.

About a month later, Gary, his wife, and even other employees became the targets of a vicious social media attack from an unknown Twitter account. This account was only a few days old, had few followers, and had been apparently set up for the sole purpose of damaging the reputation of Gary and anyone associated with him or his business. Dozens of tweets were sent out at all hours of the day with the most outrageous and crude accusations imaginable. Nobody was immune; even some of his followers were targeted. When the account was blocked, another was created within hours for the same purpose, and the attacks continued for several weeks. Completely baffled, no one could figure out who the cyber stalker was or what had prompted these attacks.

It was only when the attacker sent bizarre pictures attached to text messages to Gary and his wife that she was unveiled. It was Sarah. Apparently unhappy that she had not been offered a full-time position, this socially awkward and publicly shy young woman had morphed into an aggressive cyber bully. The ability to lash out anonymously from behind the safety of her laptop computer gave her a vehicle for expressing emotions (albeit in a nonconstructive manner) that she couldn't share face to face. Even though nobody responded to any of her tweets (the approach most frequently recommended by experts), it finally took intervention by local law enforcement officials to bring the attacks to an end.

Diminishing Breadth of Perspectives in the Digital Age

Tangentially related to the last example, the emergence of our digital society is changing both what we see and how we see it. While the explosive growth of the Internet has unquestionably resulted in benefits without which most of us would now feel handicapped (up-to-the minute news, online shopping, instantaneous communication with anyone we know), it has also resulted in unanticipated challenges. We have unprecedented access to news and information on almost any topic imaginable, but we also have the ability to match the interpretation and commentary on this information to neatly fit our predominant world view. In contrast, past generations got their news from the same major print reporting outlets and television networks, most which strived for neutrality and objectivity. Now there are literally hundreds of broadcast and online news channels from which to choose, many with intentional political or religious bias.

A great example of this phenomenon was on display in the fall of 2012. In the run to the U.S. presidency between Mitt Romney and Barack Obama, television viewers were subjected to a barrage of negative ads on virtually all channels (especially if you lived in one of the "battleground" states). But the tone of analysis and commentary on each channel was different, both in the weeks leading up to the election and on election night itself. As the state-by-state vote counts were being reported and analyzed, each channel had a slightly different tone and slant. Viewers who tuned in to MSNBC, PBS (via member stations), or Fox had very different contextual backdrops for watching essentially the same information. Fox News, with its intentionally conservative orientation, notably stood apart from other major networks with its questioning of Barack Obama's apparent victories in battleground states Wisconsin and Ohio (and the overall election). Writing for the U.K.-based news outlet *The Guardian*, Ed Pilkington offered the following analysis of this shift in viewer perceptions and preference:

> *The motto of the [Fox News] network is "fair and balanced," but in many respects it is anything but. "Fox News is not really a news network, it's a commentary network. Its news output is a small island in a vast sea of very conservative commentary," said Mike Hoyt, editor of the Columbia Journalism Review whose March issue features a cover story exploring the Fox News phenomenon.*
>
> *The poll findings underline the partisan nature of both the network and its audience. When the respondents are broken down by party affiliation, an overwhelming 74 percent of Republican-leaning Americans trust the network, but only 30 percent of Democrats.[1]*

As it pertains to the topic of respect, it would appear that this shift away from a common, objective presentation of news and ideas is leading to a hardening of our attitudes. Once we land on a particular orientation of how the world is or should be, it is all too easy to spoon-feed ourselves an unbalanced diet of new information that minimizes dissonance and further reinforces our existing beliefs. The resulting absence of well-thought-out, opposing views makes it all more likely that we attach a sense of moral correctness to our perspectives. It's easy enough to convince ourselves that we're right when we're left alone. When you add a chorus of others (including public figures and celebrities) who espouse similar beliefs, our sense of correctness can become almost airtight.

It is this self-created and self-sustaining (through the media) polarization that subsequently encourages us to demonize those who do not share our beliefs. When we believe that others are either intellectually wrong or morally flawed, the doorway to disrespect unlocks itself as "they" become our enemies. We then rationalize to ourselves that we shouldn't listen to our enemies because they lie. We shouldn't compromise with them because they won't compromise with us. No, enemies must be fought and, God willing (because we're "right"), defeated.

> Yep, son, we have met the enemy, and he is us.
>
> Pogo (cartoon character by Walt Kelly, 1971)

Exacerbated by our frequently used ability to fine-tune our news inputs, common ground and ideological compromise seem to be on a trajectory to becoming relics of a bygone era. The list of respected political moderates, such as Steven LaTourette (R-Ohio) and Olympia Snowe (R-Maine), who made the decision to leave Congress because of the stifling level of partisanship, is evidence of this trend. And while it would be convenient to blame the remaining politicians for the growing political gridlock, the real culprits may be closer to home. If the political system in the United States is polarized to the point of being dysfunctional, maybe it's simply a reflection of those of us who voted our current elected officials into office.

Digital Blindness

While not related to the media, there is another obstacle to respect that is a direct by-product of the digital age. It's the very nature of how we now communicate with one another today. Ever since humans first developed the ability to communicate with each other, our ability to share information, ideas, knowledge, and opinions has gone through a breathtaking series of transformations. But like most histories of transformation, some elements of change have had unintended consequences.

Approximately 200,000 years ago, our ancestors' grunts and howls gave way to the spoken word: language and stories. And it wasn't until 30,000 years ago that language (still rudimentary by today's standards) was augmented by pictures and symbols, either carved or painted onto cave walls. This breakthrough marked a significant expansion in capability for the human brain because it permitted the nonverbal communication of information through time. These elements eventually led to pictograms (12,000 BC), hieroglyphs (6000 BC), and the first written "words" in the form of cuneiform (2600 BC). The written word quickly became the printed word, which, with the help of Johannes Gutenberg, and his invention of printing, became the published word starting in AD 1450.

Even with increasingly efficient publishing technology, the vast majority of our communication with each other was still face-to-face, even after telephones became a common household tool. Because of this, humans could continue to rely upon their exceptional abilities to interpret both auditory and visual cues to help them accurately decode the message from sender to receiver. While the connection between nonverbal communication and respect is discussed in more detail later, it's important to note that the use of hand gestures, eye movement, body position, tone, speed, and volume of voice has been an invaluable part of our communication process since before humans learned to speak. Now, in the span of less than 25 years, technology is radically altering this process, Ironically, for all the speed and efficiency that e-mail, instant messaging, texting, and tweeting provide, we now struggle with what they prevent. Starting with the widespread use of telephones in the 1920s, we have gradually stripped away many of the communication "clues" that are built in to face-to-face communication. While telephone conversations at least convey tone, volume, speed, and so on, typed communication vehicles like e-mail strip away everything but the written word. When you move to vehicles such as text messages and tweets, even the number of words used to convey ideas, wants, and intentions becomes drastically limited. Each time you strip away some of the communication clues that we have relied upon for over 200,000 years, the opportunity for misinterpretation increases dramatically. What the sender intends to convey versus what the receiver interprets and believes can be worlds apart. In many cases, innocent messages are misunderstood, and disrespectful intentions are assumed.

Digital blindness can eventually give way to digital detachment. Because we cannot see or hear the emotional impact of our digital messages on recipients in real time, we are much less inclined (or even able) to filter what and how we communicate through the powerful lens of human empathy. How can someone know they've offended another without the telltale look of rejection or resentment that would be present in face-to-face communication? Even in phone conversations, there are clues to the emotions such as excitement as a daughter shares a story about camp, silence after a boyfriend says he wants to date others, or sadness as a friend shares that his family had to put their dog to sleep. These clues are typically missing in the vast majority of digital exchanges.

As a father and an educator, my biggest concern with the exponential growth of digital messaging limited to a few sentences or 140 characters is that our children (and some adults) increasingly prefer it to face-to-face communication. And why wouldn't they? It's intellectually easier to not have to consider others emotions before you speak (or text or tweet). Breaking up with a boyfriend or girlfriend by text message is relatively painless compared to doing it in person or over the phone. Posting hurtful comments on someone's Facebook page or sending slanderous tweets from phony Twitter profiles is not only common, but the anonymity is making them the preferred mode of bullying.

What will the long-term consequences for today's "digital natives" be? It's hard to tell, but evolution is a very predictable in one sense. We either use it or lose it. If more and more of our communication is done in ways that suppress empathy and otherwise disconnect us from the emotional impact of what we say, something will be lost. If we're not careful, the very capacity for respecting one another may be one of the first casualties.

Alpha Males and the Chemistry of Aggression

Even if not sociopathic, it's long been observed that a small minority of men (and some women) demonstrate a pattern of dominance-related (alpha) behaviors around both each other and members of the opposite sex. The qualities that are typically associated with people belonging to this category include physical strength, physical size, relative attractiveness, and possibly higher base-level intelligence. From an evolutionary perspective, the "alphas" from both genders would presumably be the most desirable mates for ensuring the success of their genes. Amusingly, a simple Google search on the term "alpha male traits" returns dozens of websites or resources that offer to teach would-be Romeos how to behave like *real* alpha men. One such site leads with the following assertion:

> One of the Alpha Male characteristics, a very important one, is that he displays confidence and dominance. He leads others and is ahead of the game all the time. He doesn't ask, he tells.[2]

Interestingly, there may actually be a chemical component to the whole "alpha" behavior set. Higher levels of the hormone testosterone have been linked to myriad antisocial behaviors, such as aggression (including rage) and selfishness. Chemically, testosterone inhibits the bonding of oxytocin to receptor sites in the body which makes us simultaneously more aggressive, less trusting, and less empathetic to the emotional experiences of others. Unfortunately, there are significant downsides to an excess of testosterone in our systems. For men in particular, it is linked to learning disabilities, higher divorce rates, more job changes, being viewed socially as overcompetitive, and persistent states of anger and frustration.[3]

Selfishness and Self-Interest

Let's face it; we have all behaved selfishly at one time or another. In part, this capacity is genetically wired into human DNA as an element relating to our survival in a world with historically limited resources. In past generations, and currently in many parts of the world, the acquisition of food or other material resources for one person, at the expense of another, meant a better chance of long-term survival for that one person and that person's offspring. It was this basic line of reasoning that led to the concept of *rational self-interest*. First articulated by Adam Smith (*The Theory of Moral Sentiments*) in 1759, this notion hypothesizes that human beings will almost always behave in ways that maximize their satisfaction and/or well-being, even if it comes at the expense of others. The strength of this orientation would presumably be stronger if the "expense" came from others who were more physically or emotionally removed from us.

Not only did this notion become the basic assumption for behaviors in a capitalist economy, but it was also expanded upon and reinforced almost to the point of irrefutability by John Forbes Nash in his

1951 article "Non-Cooperative Games."[4] Even though since deemed unreliable in many scenarios, the so-called Nash equilibrium asserted that individuals and organizations would almost always behave in ways that would maximize their own gain. Whether their actions helped or harmed other parties was coincidental and purely part of the strategy for maximizing their personal wealth. Frighteningly, there is some evidence suggesting that this capacity for cold calculation starts to develop very early on. In a recent article published in *PLOS ONE* by Kristin Lyn Leimgruber and colleagues from Yale University, she noted:

> *Children as young as five are generous when others are aware of their actions, but antisocial when sharing with a recipient who can't see them. Much like the patterns of charity we see in adults, donation tendencies in children appear to be driven by the amount of information available to others about their actions—for both adults and children, the more others know about their actions, the more likely they are to act generously.*[5]

With this notion of assumed self-interest positioned as a foundational truth at the heart of capitalist economic theory throughout much of the 1950s, 1960s, and 1970s, it is not difficult to see how raw capitalism could be seen as a dark, negative force by many. It's also easy to see how the "greed is good" mantra of Michael Douglas's Gordon Gekko character (from the 1987 film *Wall Street*) could lead to idolizing and encouraging economic behaviors that were rooted in ruthless self-interest.

Fortunately, Hollywood and Wall Street are infants on the evolutionary timeline and do not accurately represent our evolutionary past. When our species first adopted more advanced, tribal characteristics, we began to demonstrate behaviors that perpetuated group survival. Somehow, our brains made the connection that some degree of "we" had a better chance of survival than "me."

This complex evolutionarily insight was the origin of the first *social contracts* and the *prosocial* behaviors we now link to exchange theory. Fast-forward to modern times, and our brains still operate on the same instinctive instruction set.

> Good leaders make people feel that they're at the very heart of things, not at the periphery.
>
> Warren G. Bennis,
> American Scholar, Organizational Consultant and Author

Informing our decisions as to how we should treat others, our brains are constantly calculating our interaction strategies, executed in fractions of a second, based upon the imagined outcomes and "rewards" for specific behaviors. One example of how this capacity for calculation may have shaped our behavioral norms involves our biological instruction set to find mates and reproduce. When in the presence of females, it is widely believed that our prehistoric male ancestors were more likely to demonstrate prosocial behaviors such as sharing resources, reining in overt aggression, and treating others with compassion and kindness. The rationale for this is that, in addition to benefiting the tribe at large, females would be more likely to select males with these qualities because they would make better long-term mates and fathers.

Unfortunately, there were (and are) both environmental and social forces that discourage prosocial behaviors. When we perceive ourselves to be at a deficit in some way, especially with elements related to physical survival or social acceptance/recognition, it potentially makes it more difficult to engage others in a way that communicates respect unless we can link that respect to our own future rewards. Although not particularly flattering, it is in our nature to calculate the future value of treating others with respect.

You're Not One of Us

Much research has been conducted on the subject of group affiliation and status. As it pertains to respect, we are much more likely to treat others in ways that communicate value if we perceive that they are, somehow, like us. This *in-group* designation can be based on ethnicity, gender, geography, employer, social-economic status, political or religious affiliation, or just about any other group identifier. Regardless of whether inclusion in the group is superficial (i.e., employer) or based on genetics (skin color), controlled experiments consistently show that we are more courteous, generous, and empathetic toward those with whom we share some meaningful common bond.[6]

What about those we categorize as being from *out-groups*; those who are *not* like us and whose values and beliefs are either uncertain or suspect? Keeping in mind that we can observe, categorize, and mentalize (infer perspectives and motives) about observable differences in others in less than a second, it's safe to say that most (or at least many) of our interactions with these individuals are instinctual at first and later rationalized. We tell ourselves stories about others and their intentions and then, accurately or inaccurately, act out the appropriate response accordingly.

Stereotypes, Myths, and Assumptions

A few years ago, a colleague of mine shared a personal story with me that perfectly demonstrated just how quickly our brains can fall back on outdated, inaccurate stereotypes that can result in disrespectful behaviors and comments. "Tanya" was the director of diversity and inclusion for a highly renowned health insurance provider in the Midwest. She's tall, attractive, the mother of two boys, and extremely intelligent. In fact, she's one of the smartest professionals I have known in her position. She's also African American.

One evening, she and her husband were attending a social event for parents at their oldest son's school. He was a freshman at one of the city's more prestigious private, all boys prep schools. Mingling with the other parents at the event, they ended up talking with and introducing themselves to a number of new people. In one group, there were three other couples chatting, drinking wine, and sharing stories. All were white. When Tanya and her husband introduced themselves, they were greeted warmly and welcomed by the others, who introduced themselves as well. Most of the men included references to who they worked for and what they did. Sounding genuinely pleased to meet two of them, one of the women smiled warmly and said, "It's so nice to meet the both of you; you're such nice people. I had no idea that the school offered financial aid!"

Okay, freeze the scene. What are the different ways that this situation could play itself out? Fortunately for all involved, neither Tanya nor her husband were strangers to ignorance—even when it was dressed in cocktail attire. Almost feeling sorry for the woman's husband, who looked mortified by her comment, Tanya smiled and pleasantly replied, "You know, I don't think they do, but what a great idea. It costs a small fortune to send your kids here! I'm sure some parents could really use the help." Situation diffused, but I wish I could have been a fly on the wall to hear what the white woman's husband had to say to her in private later that night.

Is this example extreme? Probably not. It was simply more memorable because the white woman involved actually articulated (albeit unconsciously) her own stereotypical idea that a family of color would need financial assistance to send its son to the same private school that hers attended. Fortunately, experience had equipped Tanya with the perspective, temperament, and wisdom to handle what could have been interpreted as a tremendously disrespectful comment with grace, poise, and even compassion. I've asked myself many times, if the tables were turned and it had been me, how would I have responded? My respect for her grows every time I think about it.

Whether based on skin color, gender, accent, perceived education level, or economic status, we all have stereotypical ideas about different groups of people. More importantly, we frequently act upon these ideas in ways that we're often not even aware of. Sometimes they show up as passing comments, subtle nonverbal cues, a repeated pattern of the kinds of people we approach at social events, or how much time we take to help someone. More often, the acts are virtually invisible. They take the form of choosing one job candidate to invite back for a second interview over another, soliciting ideas and opinions from this person but not that one, choosing to invest extra time and attention to mentor him but not her, or recognizing the improvements of in one supervisor's department but not another's. The best defense against these almost imperceptible demonstrations of bias is to be aware of the stories we tell ourselves that allow them to happen.

Stressed Out

Stress over life's unanticipated challenges, temporary loss of perspective, feelings of powerlessness, or simply lack of enough sleep can all lead us to act disrespectfully to others—even for those of us who know better. I was recently on a late-evening business flight from Atlanta, Georgia to Jacksonville, Florida, when I had my own "respect accident," so to speak. Once I had boarded the plane and took my seat, my wife called, and I became completely absorbed in the ensuing phone conversation. Her father had unexpectedly passed away recently, and I was doing my absolute best to listen, let her vent, and otherwise be supportive.

Evidently, I had become a little too absorbed in our conversation because I did not notice that the aircraft door had been shut and that the flight attendant had asked passengers to turn off their mobile phones. I was abruptly jerked back to reality when a fellow passenger from a row ahead of me turned around, glared at me and gruffly barked, "Hey you, shut your damn phone off!"

Probably more in response to his aggressive tone than anything, I reacted instead of responding. "Shut the hell up [or something similar] and mind your own damn business," I yelled back at him. "Not that it's any concern of yours, but I'm talking to my wife whose father just died!"

Needless to say, we quickly had the attention of just about everyone within a few rows of us (but fortunately nobody from the flight crew). It didn't end there. Not dissuaded by my similarly aggressive response, my well-intentioned copassenger retorted, "I don't care why you're on the phone. The flight attendant told everyone to power down, and that includes you."

At this point, the fact that he was actually quite correct in his assertion was beside the point. With cortisol surging and adrenaline pumping, I leaned across the aisle and hissed back at him, "So unless you're a flight attendant yourself, I'll say it again: Shut the hell up and keep your nose in your own damn business!" Who was this disrespectful and caustic person that I had turned into? All 205 pounds of me was physically ready to fight—all over a request, albeit rudely delivered, that I turn my cell phone off.

Fortunately, the cabin lights dimmed, the jets roared to life, and the plane was soon airborne. Not another word was said, and the situation passed. That powerful cocktail of fight-or-flight hormones subsided and my prefrontal cortex came back online. The rage gave way to more reasoned thought, and I began to reflect on what had just transpired. As I glanced around, none of the other passengers seemed to be paying much attention anymore. I, on the other hand, was profoundly bothered by my own behavior. I felt both guilty and embarrassed. While it's safe to say that more sleep on my part and a friendlier tone in the "reminder" from my fellow passenger would likely have averted the entire incident. It was a stark reminder of how quickly stress and the perception of a hostile environment can coax normally respectful people into behaviors that are not.

When Disrespect Turns to Hostility

In the extreme, members of out-groups may become categorized as not only different from us, but potentially less than us; less intelligent, less moral, and less worthy. If you're not like me, then you're not as "good" as me. And if you're not as good me, then you may be a threat to me. And if I think you're a potential threat to me, I will keep you at arm's length or even be hostile toward you. In his powerfully written book, *Less than Human*, David Livingstone Smith explores the origins and impact of how categorizing our "enemies" as subhuman has permitted ordinary people to engage in not simply disrespectful, but downright heinous behavior.

> *Dehumanization is a scourge and has been for millennia. It acts as a psychological lubricant, dissolving our inhibitions and inflaming our destructive passions. As such, it empowers us to perform acts that would, under other circumstances, be unthinkable.*[7]

Unfocused Disrespect

Sometimes, disrespect doesn't need a direct victim. In his wonderful work titled, *The Civility Solution: What to Do When People are Rude*, Professor P. M. Forni coined the term "unfocused rudeness" to describe a pattern of disrespectful behaviors that are becoming more and more common in our society. They're behaviors that often go unchallenged because they're not directed at any of us individually. Examples of this type of behavior include people talking on their cell phones (or just texting) in the middle of a movie, someone playing music loud enough to bother others, aggressive drivers who put others at risk by weaving in and out of traffic lanes to save a few minutes, and coworkers who routinely show up late or unprepared for meetings. While these behaviors are often not directed at any one person, they harm us all because of the inconvenience they cause and the bad feelings they generate. Perhaps more insidiously, they erode the invisible bonds that link us humans.

Sometimes these behaviors are not witnessed in person, although evidence of them is on display for all to see. Consider public toilets that are left unflushed or with wet seats, cigarette butts, or other litter tossed from cars or left in parking lots, or a conference room left with chairs out of place, cans and wrappers left on the tables, and whiteboards left covered with meeting notes from who knows when. Then there are more thoughtless (and often illegal) examples of people dumping leftover lawn chemicals and waste products into public sewers or waterways, vandalism, or the creation and launching of computer viruses. While these activities are seldom focused on specific individuals, they harm us all by creating nuisances and diminish the quality of our lives.

Given our predisposition toward self-interest, the questions we have to consciously challenge ourselves with each day are:

- What is the behavioral path related to my treatment of others that will lead to the greatest future rewards, both for me individually and "us" together?
- How wide of a net can I spread for my definition of "us"—my family, my community, my department, my company, all human beings?
- Am I willing to spend my individual time and effort today, requiring the expenditure of somewhat finite physical energy, for a potentially more prosperous and rewarding tomorrow?

Without getting too deep into the psychological discussion of altruism and our capacity for delayed gratification, it is safe to conclude that any argument for respectful behavior toward others presupposes that we can overcome more instinctual urges to satisfy our own wants and needs first. If we can see no benefit to treating others with respect, then we won't treat them with respect, at least not with any consistency.

We Don't Know What We Don't Know

We can't fix what we don't know is broken, and unfortunately for most of us, this includes our scope of awareness. While broken may be a harsh term, few of us will attain the degree of awareness about others that is required to fully treat them with respect. As the saying goes, "We go with the horse that brung us." The information we rely on in our interactions with others is based on a combination of reference points amassed over the years. In what Robert Burton, M.D., referred to as "the hidden layer,"[8] our brains create a unique blueprint of how we see the world, those around us, and ourselves.

This blueprint was in part inherited, dictated to us, and pieced together over time based on our unique interpretation of past experiences. Despite its subjective nature, it represents our truth and reality at any given moment. When we interact with others, we're not so much interacting with them as they really are, but with the data we have pieced together over time about them or people like them (race, gender, age, etc.). This information tends to be persistent. Even though we can update our mental "software," our brains find it easier to reuse what we already have. So we try to force new people and situations into old patterns (see Figure 5.1) rather than creating fresh, more appropriate, patterns. Although this approach takes less energy, it also has potential seeds of disrespect. The perceptions we have of other people are rarely completely accurate.

The human brain is a magnificent piece of work. It perceives new information at lightning quick speed and instantaneously compares it to thousands of past reference points and patterns to come up with the best matches. When we meet new people, in a

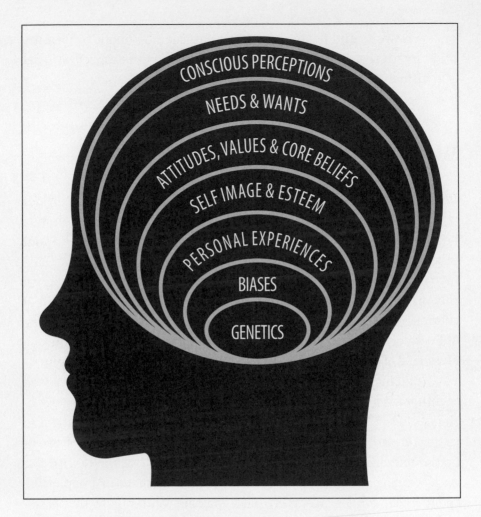

Figure 5.1   The Hidden Layer

split second we access multiple reference points that tell us about people "like them." This includes the vast spectrum of information known as stereotypes, which is defined as standardized mental pictures/models that we create for members of different groups. They can be for groups as large as "male" or as small as "trombone players." No matter what the group, most of us are able to piece together some rudimentary description of the people that belong to this group (see Figure 5.2). Contrary to what many people believe, stereotypes are not bad. They are simply tools that the brain uses

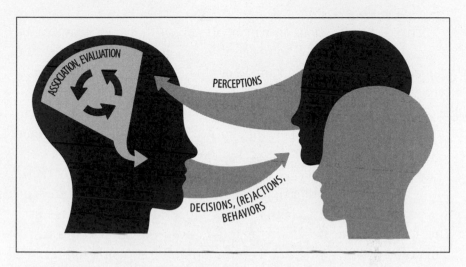

ASSOCIATION, EVALUATION

PERCEPTIONS

DECISIONS, (RE)ACTIONS, BEHAVIORS

Figure 5.2   Perceptions, Associations & Stereotypes

to efficiently categorize new reference points as quickly as possible. If it weren't for stereotypes, the amount of time and mental effort it would take us to figure out how to interact with people would make ordinary social interactions impossible. Our brains would be so busy assessing and categorizing the new data that we wouldn't have time for anything else.

As helpful as stereotypes are, they have significant and obvious limitations. Stereotypes are oversimplified pictures of the groups they describe. By their very nature, they allow no room for variation and are easily reinforced by only fragments of supporting evidence. Stereotypes reside in our minds as truths until they are displaced by new information. The only way to verify the degree to which a stereotype applies to people we associate with is through direct, one-on-one engagement.

Stereotypes by themselves would be relatively harmless except for one problem. We interact with others and take action based on stereotypes as if they were indisputable facts. In the absence of first-hand data, they're all we have to go on and so that's what we do. When we interact with people as though they are the sum of stereotypes that we've assigned to them, we are assured of being disrespectful in our approach. This mental process is the genesis of prejudice.

There are situations in which prejudicial behavior may not be damaging to the person to which it is directed, but can instead be damaging to others. An example of this is when we meet someone who we associate with a group that we have assigned favorable stereotypes such as above-average intelligence, athleticism, or particular skills or abilities. A person who graduated from an Ivy League university may be shown a preference over someone who graduated from a community college. Stereotypes often have a kernel of truth, but who's to say whether that actually makes the individual from an Ivy League university a better hire or more intelligent. The result is that a person may be shown favoritism even though it is unearned. This type of *microinequity* is common and frequently interpreted as a subtle sign of disrespect.

PART II

Tools for Building Respectful Work Cultures

CHAPTER 6 # Respect Starts with Awareness

A commitment to a respectful workplace becomes part of the fabric of an organization's culture. The greatest leverage to shape and influence culture exists at the top of an organization. Individual contributors, supervisors, and midlevel managers pay careful attention to how their senior leaders act and behave. Then, depending on their own aspirations, one of two things happens. They either try to emulate the attitudes and behaviors they think will lead to their own success or they distance themselves from the leaders they don't respect or whose behaviors they view as counterproductive. Either way, those at the top of the organization are always under the microscope. Because of this, having a clear and accurate perception of how we are viewed by others is extraordinarily important. To attempt to lead others without this vantage point is, at best, a quick road to mediocrity. At worst, it is a recipe for disaster.

The Gift of Feedback

One of the easiest ways to understand how we are perceived by others is to participate in a 360-degree feedback process. This process reveals perspectives from all levels of the organizations—from above, from peers, and from those who report to us. As long as the 360-degree feedback process is administered by skilled practitioners and used only for feedback (never for performance reviews), these instruments can provide valuable feedback that helps leaders and managers better understand how they impact the performance of those around them. While there are many solid 360-degree tools available, what's most important is that the tool selected capture the emotional impact that leaders and managers have on those around them. Do they treat people in ways that increase commitment to the organization and build employee capabilities, or do they alienate employees and diminish their long-term potential?

> All meaningful and lasting change starts on the inside and works its way out.
>
> Bob Moawad, Author and Founder of Edge Learning Institute

Getting the commitment from some leaders to participate in a 360-degree feedback process is difficult. It amazes me how many senior leaders come up with excuses for why they can't participate. Some claim it is a waste of time; that it's not important what their subordinates think. Others say they already know what people around them think, so they don't need a survey. In most cases, this type of resistance can be interpreted as a sign of fearfulness and vulnerability. These emotions are understandable; the first step is the scariest. The reward for opening ourselves up to honest feedback is priceless in its value to our future success.

The Power of Humility

In the fall of 2011, "Tom," CEO of one of the world's most successful restaurant chains, set in motion a leadership development initiative that had the impact of supercharging his entire 250-person leadership team. Having recently returned to actively leading the company he had founded years earlier, he connected with his leaders in a way that was both courageous and meaningful. For the first time in his career, Tom participated in his own 360-degree feedback process and received candid feedback from 11 others within the organization about his behaviors and leadership style. He also learned about the feelings they had about him as a leader.

Opening ourselves up to this level of feedback, at least initially, is an act of courage. It's courageous because it brings all our observable flaws into the open and makes us exceptionally vulnerable. It is this vulnerability, ironically, that has the potential to make a strong leader even stronger.

The feedback that Tom received from his team was similar to what would be expected from other senior leaders. There were some things he did very well and others that needed work. This might be the end of the story, but for one exception. Most 360-degree participants share their results only with their own bosses and maybe an executive coach. They then create an action plan that tries to leverage their strengths and improve in the areas needed. In some cases, they may share their action plans with those who provided them feedback. Tom did something quite different. He publicly shared his results with the top 250 leaders who were being tasked with helping to transform the restaurant chain and prepare it for success in the upcoming decade.

This public display of candor and humility was one of the greatest demonstrations of respect for his managers that a senior leader in his position could have offered. The respect and trust that it showed he had for those who reported to him, as one observer noted, "Literally set the group on fire." As depicted in Figure 6.1, courage led to vulnerability, which was interpreted as humility. Humility then bred trust, communicated profound respect, and significantly boosted engagement.

Most importantly, all of the company's stakeholders have benefitted from this seemingly simple act. Customers are happy, as reflected by revenue growth, employee engagement scores are up, and stockholders have been rewarded handsomely with a 65 percent increase in the share price of their stock in the six months following.

continued

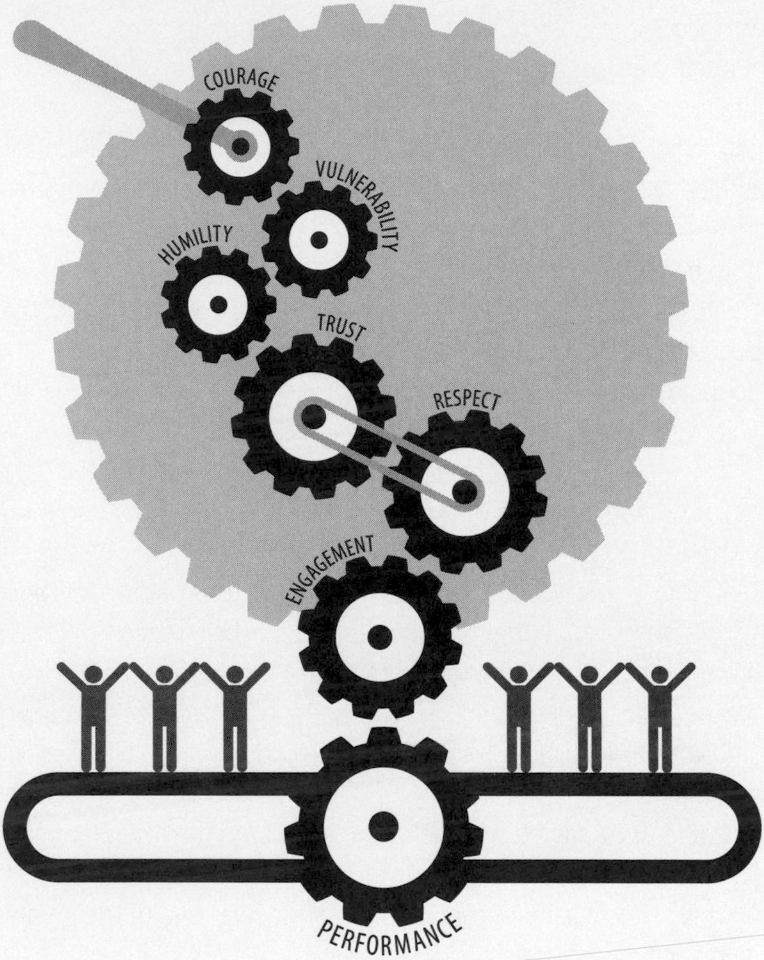

Figure 6.1   The Courageous Leader

The Power of Trust

A man who doesn't trust himself can never really trust anyone else.

Jean Francois Paul De Gondi, Cardinal de Retz,
French Churchman, Writer

One of the most important assets created by respectful leaders is trust. Trust leads to the perception of safety, and the feeling of safety helps stimulate organizational potential. Even when the environment outside an organization is in flux from the economy, competition, or changing technology, trust that coworkers and leaders will look out for each other's best interest and be truthful creates a type of stability that will endure against outside pressures. The simplest way to create trust is to pursue an unconditional policy of doing the "right thing" at every level within the organization. Although this is a simple concept, it is often difficult to implement because doing the "right thing" may require us to subordinate what's in our individual best interest. Consider the following true example.

In November, 2008 the United States and much of the rest of the world were still at the front end of what would prove to be the greatest and most prolonged recession since the Great Depression. While few industries were unaffected, manufacturing was hit disproportionately hard. With layoffs at record levels, consumers' appetite for durable goods dwindled to a mere trickle. This not only affected direct manufacturers of consumer products, but also most of their tier-one and tier-two suppliers. One such company was Metaullics Systems in Solon, Ohio, a division of Pyrotek, Incorporated. Metaullics Systems manufactured high-end mixing and pumping equipment for molten aluminum, and its products were used all over the world.

The recession hit Metaullics hard. With its revenue off by nearly 60 percent, it was forced to make deep cuts to its staffing levels. How this process was implemented allowed the company to boost morale and commitment while increasing per/employee productivity. Rich Henderson, the plant's operations manager, followed a policy of complete transparency with company employees. Revenue, customer orders, backorders, and inventory turn information were all regularly shared at the company's town hall meetings. Even in difficult times, he followed this policy religiously.

When the company's orders fell from $1.6 million to $610,000 per month (see Figure 6.2), Henderson remained candid with his employees. It was an extremely difficult time, and painful cuts were necessary. The way they were handled would be, in part, determined by the employees. While the employees at Metaullics had recently decertified their union, it was their decision to continue following union guidelines for layoffs. Any terminations would be made only after contractors were first let go. An offer was made to bridge any employees who were close to retirement. By the time the cuts were complete, almost 40 percent of the company's employees had lost their jobs. The number would have been higher except that several employees offered to initiate cuts in their own compensation to save some of their colleagues' jobs.

To an outside observer, what was astounding was the degree of loyalty, trust, and enthusiasm that resulted from Henderson's candor during bleak economic times. Despite orders dropping lower each month, Metaullics' employees didn't act as though their fate was in anyone's hands but their own. When there were no client

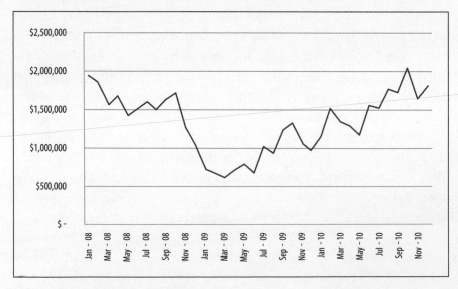

Figure 6.2   Metaullics' Shipments

orders to work on, they found other things to do. They cleaned the plant. They tackled any small repairs they could find. They caulked windows and painted walls. They did everything they could to stay productive and make the business better prepared and more efficient when the anticipated recovery arrived.

As with most businesses, the recovery finally found its way to Metaullics. Not only did the company regain its original level of client orders, but it actually increased them by over 20 percent and did it with 10 percent fewer employees. Just as importantly, it emerged with the enthusiasm, hope, and commitment of its most valuable employees intact.

How do you cultivate trust in organizations? As with most worthy pursuits, building trust isn't easy. The first step involves a shift in agendas by senior leaders. In alignment with traditional organization models, most leaders and senior managers see themselves at the top of their respective organizational hierarchies. By design, it is presumed that their jobs are to develop objectives and map out strategies for growing the business. Even if not stated, the implication is that everyone else is there to support the leaders' agenda and help execute the resulting plans. Employees are tools, sometimes affectionately referred to as human assets, to be utilized as efficiently as possible.

Organizational cultures that emerge under this human asset model don't typically develop high levels of organic trust. On the scale of priorities, employees are secondary to business goals. To grow trust, managers and leaders need to flip this model on its head and put the success and well-being of their employees squarely in the middle of their business agendas. Structurally, this is sometimes referred to as the servant leadership model,[1] where leaders are at the bottom of their organizational hierarchies. When this happens, manager and leader behaviors change because their motivations change. Successfully adopting and supporting the agendas of those below them become part of the metrics by which the leaders are evaluated.

Trust Made Simple

During a recent workshop for the sales and marketing leadership team of a Fortune 50 chemical company, one senior leader shared a story about trust that he attributed to one of his former bosses. In his words, the man conducted his life by simple and powerful values. When it came to how to lead others, only two questions needed to be answered:

1. Would your mother be proud?
2. How would you feel if someone were to ask your son or daughter to do the same thing?

Respect Through Osmosis

In a workforce that increasingly reflects the demographic differences within the population, getting people from dissimilar ages, genders, and ethnic backgrounds to work together collaboratively can be a real challenge. When you add differences in core values, moral codes, and political leanings, it can prove to be almost impossible. While most people intellectually "get" the concept that diversity of ideas and opinions should lead to creative approaches and solutions, pervasive stereotypes and the lack of familiarity and trust can create emotional roadblocks that inhibit true synergistic thinking. Until team members make the effort to work through their differences and discover their similarities, the required element of trust will remain elusive. What's a manager to do?

Never hire or promote in your own image. It is foolish to replicate your strength. It is idiotic to replicate your weakness.

Dee Hock, Founder of Visa Credit Card Association

Fortunately, the fields of psychology and organizational development can provide insight. Specifically, the principal of *contact hypothesis* holds that people who are fundamentally different from each other in significant ways (race, age, social values, etc.) can work through prejudices and be coaxed into working together collaboratively under the right conditions. This can be accomplished even if the differences have led to a state of conflict. The most important factors for this principle to work are:

- All substantial sources of conflict be dealt with or removed.
- All individuals have equal power, stature, and privileges.
- The members of the overall group should be given a task that can't be accomplished successfully unless all members work together (structured interdependence).
- The environment in which the "contact" takes place is neutral and conducive to positive, friendly interactions.

Ideally, contact hypothesis leads to higher levels of group productivity and the dilution of negative stereotypes that different members may have toward each others' groups.

Respect as a Global Value

Corporate giant E.I. DuPont de Nemours and Company (DuPont), the Delaware-based diversified manufacturer, have four core values. The first three are safety, exhibiting the highest ethical standards, and protecting the environment. When the company included respect for people as the fourth, it was onto something. DuPont realized a long time ago that if you respect your people, they will respect each other, produce at a higher level, and improve in the other three core values. For these reasons, respect has been a company core value for years. While there may be a peripheral impact on profits and litigation avoidance,

continued

these are coincidental. DuPont leadership believes it's the right way to run a successful company.

According to Greg Martz, director of respect for people central, "Though we had a diverse, inclusive work environment, our other core values had more structure, systemized improvement programs, and dedicated resources. Respect for people was trailing in its formal approach." In 2009 DuPont's senior leadership decided to do something about it.

The effort started with a survey of over 13,000 of DuPont's 58,000 employees in 69 locations. The results of this enormous undertaking showed that close to 90 percent of those surveyed believed that DuPont was a respectful place to work. That would be a satisfactory mark for many organizations, but in terms of a core value within DuPont, 90 percent left room for improvement. Company leaders knew they needed training, audit capabilities, metrics, and communications processes.

With the direction of Legacy Business Cultures, who helped with the creation of a customized training curriculum, DuPont trained over 200 facilitators worldwide by the summer of 2011. DuPont is committed to delivering respect training in 25 languages to more than 40,000 employees by 2014. Senior leadership at DuPont fully supports the effort and is providing the resources and funding to ensure that the major corporate roll will be successful.

Along with the training, DuPont is also creating internal communications programs that help generate more knowledge about respect. DuPont is convinced that the effort it is championing will make it a better place to work and provide a positive bottom line return. That's good news for both employees and the company's shareholders.[2]

CHAPTER 7 # The 12 Rules of Respect

As previously mentioned, respect is demonstrated in different ways and practiced one interaction at a time. The 12 rules of respect discussed in this chapter illustrate ways of thinking and behaving around others. They have been shown to be tremendously powerful at positively affecting how people perceive both others and themselves when interacting.

1. Be Aware of Your Nonverbal and Extra-verbal Cues

Whenever we are interacting in person with others, we are deploying and responding to multiple modes of communication. First, there are the words themselves. Language is a tool of nuance, and using the right words to create the desired meaning can be an important skill that we learn over the course of our lives. Even more critical than the actual words are the countless nonverbal and extra-verbal cues we employ to deliver the words. The simple phrase, "We should probably talk about this," can mean any number of things depending on how it is said.

Psychologist Albert Mehrabian is often quoted for suggesting that as much as 93 percent of the messaging that occurs between individuals when talking in person transpires through nonverbal and extra-verbal cues. This is not to suggest that words are inconsequential, but rather that the interpretation of our true intent is more accurately determined by the way in which our words are delivered. Extra-verbal cues include the speed with which we speak, our volume relative to background noise, our inflection, and our willingness to pause to make space for others to speak. Nonverbal cues can be subtle, such as physical proximity to those with whom we speak. Obvious nonverbal cues can include hand gestures, eye movements, and facial expressions. It is important to remember that when our nonverbal and extra-verbal cues appear to convey a different message from our words, the human brain is programmed to give more credence to the nonverbal.

> We often refuse to accept an idea merely because the tone of voice in which it has been expressed is unsympathetic to us.
>
> Friedrich Nietzsche, German Philosopher, Poet, Composer

If we're trying to communicate respect, it's critical that we minimize the occurrence of cues that suggest otherwise. Behaviors such as yelling, rolling our eyes, shaking our head in opposition, interrupting, sighing, avoiding eye contact, frowning, and foot tapping can't be ignored, no matter how respectful our actual words may be. That is why it is a critical skill to synchronize all our communication modes to deliver the same message.

Technology plays an increasing role in contributing to misunderstandings among people, including the unintended perception of disrespect. Despite the benefits we derive from e-mailing, texting, posting, and tweeting, there is a dark side. When we strip away the accompanying delivery cues that human beings have evolved, our electronically delivered words can take on a life of their own. Because *intended* meaning can easily be trumped by *assumed* meaning, it is best to utilize face-to-face communication whenever the subject or message has the potential of evoking emotions. When in-person communication isn't possible, a phone call is the next best option.

2. Develop Curiosity About the Perspectives of Others

Like many people, I woke up this morning knowing exactly how the world was—at least according to me. I knew which faith was the right faith, which political party could successfully lead our country into the future, and what social values were best for America. That's my story, and I'm sticking to it. Okay, not exactly, but you get the point. As each of us navigates our way through the twists and turns of life, love, and business, we do so from our unique perspectives. What we usually don't do, however, is explore the perspectives of others, even when they're on similar journeys.

> Most of the successful people I've known are the ones who do more listening than talking.
> Bernard M. Baruch, American Financier and Political Consultant

Empathy, defined as the ability to understand the emotional position of others, starts with curiosity and is demonstrated through active inquiry. For example:

- I wonder how Adam might feel about that.
- I wonder what made Sue respond that way.

- How is Carl likely to respond when I share my idea?
- I wonder what I could do to make Tamika feel better.

Sometimes we silently ask ourselves the questions. Other times we speak out loud to those in our presence. Either way, empathy is demonstrated when it becomes evident to others around us that we are interested in what they think, why they think it, and how they feel about it. When this happens, it becomes easier to communicate respect to others, even if we disagree with them.

3. Assume That Everyone Is Smart About Something

While assumptions can sometimes get us into trouble, there is one that usually doesn't. Whenever I'm meeting someone for the first time, or even a new group of people, I like to assume that each one of them is intelligent in his or her own way. Because I like to think I'm smart, it is reasonable to assume that other people like to think they also are smart. The only difference is that we are all smart through different histories and life experiences.

> Everyone is a genius. But if you judge a fish on its ability to climb a tree, it will live its whole life feeling stupid.
>
> Albert Einstein, Theoretical Physicist

My story is unique to me. I grew up in a suburb of Columbus, Ohio. I went to parochial schools and then on to graduate from The Ohio State University. While I was at OSU, I interned with two well-known companies and joined one as a full-time employee after graduation.

From there, I moved to Colorado and then Oregon before settling in the Cleveland, Ohio area. Along the way, I earned an MBA and, in 1997, left the safe cubicles of a Fortune 50 company to start my own business. Although there are undoubtedly other people in the world who grew up in Columbus, moved out of state, moved back to Ohio and started their own company, the pool is small and the nuances great.

Since 1997, I've worked on five continents and presented my ideas to over a quarter of a million business leaders and professionals. Because of this unique journey, I became fairly smart in my particular fields of expertise. This does not make me smarter than others around me, just smart in a different way. That's the way it is with most people. Others that we meet are smart, only their stories are different, and they became smart through different life experiences. What about you? How did you get smart? More importantly, how does it feel when the people you work with treat you as if you are smart?

4. Become a Better Listener by Shaking Your "But"

Words are tools of nuance. They are not good or bad; they are merely tools, and knowing which words to use and not to use in a conversation can make a big difference. One word in particular can be used in a way that hinders our ability to show respect. That word is "but." While it's difficult to imagine any conversation of length without using this word, when and how we use it have a tremendous impact in communicating whether or not we value someone's opinion and ideas.

Coming from a large family, I'm familiar with the "yeah, but" phenomenon. It goes something like this: You're having a conversation with someone, typically about a subject that both of you have different opinions on, like whose turn it is to host Thanksgiving dinner this year. When one person gets halfway through explaining his or her position, the other jumps in with a "yeah, but ..." and commandeers the metaphorical microphone. Then midstream through his or her point, the courtesy is returned. After several minutes, instead of having a productive exchange of ideas and opinions, both sides are battling to have their perspective accepted, and neither party feels heard. Similar incidents take place at work, with different subjects and power dynamics.

While interrupting others is disrespectful on its own, the language that follows can make things worse. The danger with using the word "but" when discussing different ideas and perspectives is that it negates whatever came before it. As soon as your idea or opinion is presented, a "but" from someone else has the psychological impact of saying, "You're wrong." The word "however" is no better. While possibly sounding a bit more polite, it subtlety communicates the same lack of regard for what came before it. To better understand the dynamics of the word "but," consider the following exchange:

Bill: John, my team has kicked this around for over a week. As a company, we've got to do a better job of distinguishing ourselves from our competitors. If we ...

John: Yeah, but the only way to do that is to spend more money on advertising, and we just don't have that in the budget right now.

Bill: But, John, listen, there's more than one way to do this. Does advertising cost money? Sure it does, but...

John: No buts, John. The budget has been set for over six months, and we're not going to change it.

While this conversation can continue, the tone has already been set. Rather than sharing their ideas and perspectives, John and Bill are battling each other over their ideas. Little information is being shared, and both feel frustrated. If John happens to be Bill's boss, more than likely Bill feels devalued. If others were present when this exchange took place, Bill also feels embarrassed. Because of the subtle disrespect shown, the team has made no progress in solving the challenge it faces. More significantly, rather than continuing to think about ideas to address the situation, Bill has been temporarily sidelined while he deals with the emotional impact of having been treated with disrespect.

Let's rewind the exchange, eliminate the interruptions, and try to change a few of the words.

Bill: John, my team has discussed this for over a week. As a company, we've got to do a better job of distinguishing ourselves from our competitors. If we can create a higher level of visibility in our key markets and position ourselves as *the* supplier of choice, I think we can hit, and maybe event beat, our Q4 sales forecast.

John: Bill, *I hear what you're saying, and it makes a lot of sense.* A higher level of visibility within markets like Chicago and D.C. could make a huge difference for us. *At the same time,* won't we have to spend more money on advertising? All the directors, including me, are under a lot of pressure to watch budgets right now.

Bill: *You're right, John.* Advertising does cost money. *And, I hear you loud and clear* about the budget. There has been lots of gossip in the halls about belt-tightening, so I've already been thinking about ways around this challenge. What if we scaled back our trade show budget and reallocated some of that money to advertising? Some of our clients are tightening their belts also, and many aren't even going to the shows this year. They still read the trade journals, and they still listen to the radio.

John: *You know, Bill, I'd never thought about that.* I think *you might be onto something* with the shows. And with some of our competitors also scaling back budgets, I'll bet we might even be able to get ad space at a discount next quarter.

Look at the difference a few words can make. Simply by not interrupting and replacing the "buts" with words that validate and convey consideration, the entire tone changed. Without asking for it, both Bill and John received something they valued tremendously: validation. Bill got validation that his ideas were carefully thought out, and John received validation that his budget concerns were not discounted. By working together they made significant progress on their challenge and remained fully engaged in finding the best path forward. If we want to have a productive exchange of ideas in a respectful manner, then it becomes crucial that we demonstrate value for each others' positions.

> I know that you believe you understand what you think I said, but I'm not sure you realize that what you heard is not what I meant.
>
> Friedrich Nietzsche, German Philosopher, Poet, Composer

5. Look for Opportunities to Connect with and Support Others

Differences of opinion and occasional conflicts are inevitable; they are woven tightly into the fabric of the human social experience. Sometimes the source of these conflicts is clear and readily understood, as in competitions, and other times they just happen because orbits collide without warning. Such was the case my junior year in college when I was a resident advisor (RA). My first RA assignment was to serve as the resource for a group of 60 guys living in three separate wings of the dormitory. My group included a high percentage of scholarship athletes, mostly freshmen, and this was their first time living on their own. There were twelve football players, four basketball players, and two golfers on the floors. Athletes living in college dorms at an NCAA Division I school have different experiences from nonathlete students, including dissimilar schedules, access to resources, separate eating facilities, and their own "in group" behavior norms. Add a few contraband beers into the mix on weekends, and you have an interesting situation.

One Saturday evening shortly after the end of football season, I was making rounds when "Dwayne," the lone junior football player on the floor, suddenly crashed through the double doors I was about to go through, nearly knocking me into a wall. Dwayne was about 6 foot 2 inches tall, 220 pounds, and built like a freight train. I realized was that he was extremely agitated, had been drinking, and was in absolutely no mood to be messed with. "Whoa, whoa, whoa," I said, trying to defuse his anger. "Get out of my way and mind your own business," he shouted. Clearly I was in the wrong place at the wrong time. I didn't want a physical confrontation; that would not have ended well for me, but I also didn't want Dwayne to take his anger out on any of the other guys on the floor.

Primarily, out of a sense of self-preservation, I blurted out, "Dwayne, I'm not sure what happened to you tonight. Is there anything I can do to help?" Of all the things I could have said, that evidently was the right choice. Almost immediately, his demeanor changed. Dwayne stepped back, took a deep breath, and apologized. "Sorry man," he said. "It's got nothin' to do with you." I looked at him with the most empathetic look I could conjure up and continued. "Seriously, is there anything I can do to help?" At that point, the confrontation was over. Dwayne actually smiled and said, "Nah, I'll be alright. Sorry 'bout that." He shyly looked down and went back the way he came.

While I never did figure out what Dwayne was upset about, I accidentally learned a valuable lesson. Even in the heat of conflict, there are ways to connect with people if we want to. When we demonstrate a willingness to move away from our immediate agenda and search for positions of agreement first, it makes working through the actual differences a bit easier.

> The self is not something ready-made but something in continuous formation through choice of action.
>
> John Dewey, American Philospher, Phychologist, Educational Reformer

When it comes to connecting with others, one of the greatest skills we can develop is the ability to use language that lets people know it is safe for them to be themselves in our presence. This requires two things. First, we don't assume everyone is like us, even if they look like us. Second, it is genuinely okay for people to be their *complete* selves around us, regardless of the differences between us. Assuming these criteria are met, we often need to explicitly use language that reflects this. For example, if I have a devout belief in a particular religion, do I use language around others that lets them know that I hold them in high regard even if they don't share my beliefs? If I'm heterosexual with pictures of my wife and children displayed in my office, do I use language that informs my LGBT coworkers or subordinates, whose sexual orientation may be unknown to me, that it's okay for them to be the way they are? We benefit ourselves, others, and our organization when we cultivate a vocabulary that lets people know that, despite our differences, there are likely many more similarities between us.

6. When You Disagree, Explain Why

On January 28, 1986, one of the greatest space disasters in history took place in the skies off the coast of Central Florida. The space shuttle Challenger exploded 73 seconds after liftoff, taking the lives of all seven crew members. In the months that followed, what made this disaster worse was news that it could have been prevented. An internal investigation revealed that Challenger was launched that morning at a temperature lower than was approved for the O-ring seals on the shuttle booster rockets. More troubling was that several NASA engineers were aware of this before the launch and never voiced their concerns at a level that could have stopped the launch.

The drawn-out investigation revealed no malice on the part of the engineers. Rather, it discovered serious problems within NASA's culture. People were afraid to speak their mind, especially when their opinions might contradict those of their superiors. The decision to launch that morning was made at the highest levels within NASA, and nobody below wanted to stick their neck out and say, "Wait this may not be safe." The rest is history.

It is disrespectful when we fail to share our observations and opinions in order to avoid conflict. We have an obligation to others to be truthful with our perspectives and points of view. When done with civility, tact, and room for counterarguments, sharing our perspectives leads to the best decisions and optimal results. It also prevents the accumulation of "baggage" that builds up when we keep things bottled up.

The one caveat is that sharing perspectives has to go both ways. We have an obligation to share our perspectives and opinions with others, especially when safety or other important issues are involved. We also have an obligation to be good listeners. Even when we haven't asked for the opinions of others, we must demonstrate some faith in their good intentions when they present them.

7. Look for Opportunities to Grow, Stretch, and Change

It is safe to say that most of us go through life critiquing other people's actions and decisions based on our own perspectives and standards. When relationships become strained or our opinions of others become overly critical, we typically take the position that it's other people who are doing something wrong. It takes less effort to think this way, because it places the onus for improvement and change on others. As convenient (and efficient) as this may be for our brains, it can easily become an excuse for not engaging in learning, "flexing," and the personal growth that we should pursue.

An example is the dynamics in the relationship that forms between husbands and wives, partners, or significant others. The longer we are together, the more established our patterns of interaction become, and the blinder we tend to be to our own deficiencies. After five years of marriage, my wife Kim gradually began pointing out to me that I had a hard time getting out of some of my comfort zones. My original reaction was to resist this notion and insist that I could be as flexible as anyone else. But, if I could rationalize and articulate why my current way of doing things made more sense than her new ways, then there was no need for me to change. As you can imagine, this kind of logic grew tiring for my wife. It would be difficult to stay married or in a relationship with a partner that had to be dragged through life to every new opportunity. I'm happy to report that, despite my bad habits, we've been married almost 15 years. One of the reasons my wife still puts up with me is that I've gotten better at acknowledging my preference for the predictable and shown more of an appetite for tossing caution to the wind on occasion.

> Change will never happen when people lack the ability and courage to see themselves for who they are.
>
> Bryant H. McGill, Founder, Goodwill Treaty for World Peace

As we develop the desire and the willingness to hold ourselves up to the proverbial "bright light" for an occasional reality check, two things happen. First, we become infinitely easier to be around because we are less critical of others. Second, we grow in wisdom and perspective. That's because we start considering that, in situations where we might initially view others critically, the problems may be ours to deal with and not theirs.

8. Learn to Be Wrong on Occasion

My favorite of the 12 rules, and the one hardest to follow, is to learn to be wrong. Neurologist and author Robert Burton, MD, artfully captured this sentiment when he reflected on the pioneering research conducted by Social Psychologists James Carlsmith and Leon Festinger on the topic of cognitive dissonance. Festinger's seminal observation is:

> *The more committed we are to a belief, the harder it is to relinquish, even in the face of overwhelming contradictory evidence. Instead of acknowledging error in judgment and abandoning the opinion, we tend to develop a new attitude or belief that will justify retaining it.*[1]

Little did my wife know that it wasn't just me. Indeed, as a species, it appears we are more prone to rationalize than be rational. Dr. Burton went on to write that, from a neurological perspective, there is absolutely no correlation between our degree of certainty about a subject and the likelihood that we are actually correct in our beliefs. This means that our feeling of certainty about something is nothing more than a strong emotion. The stronger the emotion, the more likely we are to develop blind spots around it. While unintentional, a mindset of certainty can also set the stage for potentially disrespectful treatment of others, especially toward those who do not share our closely held beliefs.

> Let us be a little humble; let us think that the truth may not perhaps be entirely with us.
>
> Jawaharlal Nehru, First Prime Minister of India

A demonstration of our propensity to rationalize is when faith and fact collide. Think about it. We all have those hot-button topics; the ones in which our positions become emotionally entrenched, and any evidence to the contrary is discounted before it's even considered. What subjects arouse strong feelings in you—your faith, political viewpoint, position on gay marriage, or abortion? To what lengths would you go to try to get others to conform to or behave in accordance with the way you think?

An example that clearly illustrates this phenomenon is the discussion of gay rights and the nature of homosexuality in the United States. According to the 2009 Angus Reid Public Opinion survey, 47 percent of U.S. adults believed that homosexuality is a lifestyle choice. By comparison, only 34 percent of those surveyed thought that it was something with which people were born.[2] What is interesting about these statistics is that available scientific data clearly and unequivocally paint a different picture. The research on the subject is so conclusive, that it is no longer considered a subject of debate in the scientific community. Homosexuality is no more a lifestyle choice than is heterosexuality. Nor is it a disease to be cured or a mental illness to be treated. To the contrary, the American Psychiatric Association has maintained the unambiguous position since 1973 that homosexuality is not a mental illness and warns against the dangers of trying to convert gays to being straight based upon moral or religious convictions. We still live in a society in which many are too willing to ignore hard data if it allows us to "be right" about our previously held convictions.

Being willing to consider other points of view, even when we "know" we are right, is a significant demonstration of respect for others. There's a greater benefit; we open the door to learning. When we genuinely consider points of view and data that run counter to what we believe to be true, only good things can happen. We demonstrate respect for others, increase our awareness of what they think and why they think that way, and increase the likelihood that we will be able to work with them in a mutually productive manner. As U.S. social author Eric Hoffer eloquently noted, "In times of change, learners inherit the earth, while the learned are beautifully equipped to deal with a world that no longer exists."[3]

9. Never Hesitate to Say You Are Sorry

A stiff apology is a second insult. … The injured party does not want to be compensated because he has been wronged; he wants to be healed because he has been hurt.

G. K. Chesterton, English Writer

If I had a nickel for every time I've said I'm sorry, I'd be rich. If I had a nickel for every time I should have said I'm sorry, I'd be retired. No one is perfect. Even if we are normally respectful in our interactions with others, we have those moments when we don't act our best, those moments that we wish we could erase and do over. Unfortunately, it is often when we're at our worst that our actions are most memorable to others. As previously mentioned, it's the way we're wired. Disrespectful behaviors that harm us are immediately sent to long-term memory where they are stored for future reference.

Fortunately, we don't expect everybody to be perfect. We do expect people to make it right when their words, actions, or decisions cause damage. Yelling, misplaced blame, snide comments, and public ridicule all create a chemical signature that is often repeatedly replayed in the minds of the receivers unless an honest apology is offered as close to the event as possible. If it isn't, the damage can worsen. The original incident often morphs into something much worse than it actually was. Remember that the human brain typically is not very good at remembering the exact details of events. We remember the emotions and, over time, re-create (sometimes invent) the specific events to match.

When the damage is done in public, to be effective the apology must occur in the same venue. This is because of the amplification that occurs whenever we publicly praise or criticize. Admittedly, this is sometimes easier said than done. Until we get in the habit of consistently holding ourselves accountable for how we treat others, saying that we're sorry in public demonstrates courage of the highest order. But, there is a reward for that courage. Publicly admitting that we've behaved poorly and expressing remorse for our actions display vulnerability and humanness that actually make us more effective leaders.

10. Intentionally Engage Others in Ways That Build Their Self-Esteem

We have all met people who have the ability to make us feel special. It is usually the result of many small things they do. They ask questions and listen intently to our replies, smile, and nod their head in approval when we share our ideas. They applaud our efforts and point out how the things we do make a difference. On occasion, they offer feedback in order to help us become more successful. What is it that guides some people to be better at this than others? It is intention, or at least it starts there. When we interact with others with the specific goal of building their sense of worth and confidence, we look for unique ways of doing so throughout the encounter.

Building esteem in people we work with or for requires a shift in agendas. It takes a shift in focus away from what we need to what others need. While possibly feeling counterintuitive, it is the ability to make this shift that enables leaders and managers to become more influential and effective. So important is this capacity that many practitioners in the field of leadership development believe it should be a baseline requirement for promotion to senior positions. Years ago, my colleague Teresa Welborne, PhD, president of eePulse, noted during a presentation to Northeast Ohio HR leaders:

If you are in a leadership position and are not a people person, you become a liability to your organization. And if youre not willing to make the effort to become a people person, you should not be in a position of leadership.

Dr. Welborne's rationale is simple. If you're in a leadership position at any level within an organization, your number one job is to try to increase the capability and capacity of those who report to you. This focus is the surest and fastest way to improving the effectiveness of any team. Figuring out how to build each player's capacity is a one-on-one job and requires that we engage others in a manner that reflects what's important to them, not to us. As you make this investment in those who report to you, it builds trust, raises their confidence, and reaffirms their long-term value to the organization. It also takes time and energy. If being a "people person" hasn't been a priority for you, making the initial change to focus on other people's agendas may be one that takes great effort.

11. Be Respectful of Time When Making Comments

I hate to admit it. I've always been a talker. I was born that way. According to my parents, this behavior dominated my personality from about the time I was one-year-old. No matter what anybody else was talking about, my contributions needed to take center stage. It has even been rumored that my grandmother would on occasion tell me, "Paul Meshanko, there's a reason God gave you two ears and one mouth!" Now I personally find it hard to believe that my grandmother would ever have uttered those exact words to me, but it is possible.

> One of the most sincere forms of respect is actually listening to what another has to say.
>
> Bryant H. McGill, Founder, Goodwill Treaty for World Peace

Learning to share our thoughts and ideas, while making time for others to do the same, comes easier to some people than others. It requires a degree of social skill, awareness of our "position" relative to those we're speaking with, and communication skills that allow us to tactfully and proportionally make our points. More than these skills, the ability to interact consistently with others equitably comes from our attitudinal predispositions toward them. Specifically, we need to continue to cultivate both curiosity and value for the perspectives of others. If we don't become curious or have value for what other people have to say, it is difficult to consistently fake the behaviors that demonstrate interest.

12. Smile!

Sometimes the most effective strategies are also the simplest. With rare exception, when we meet people who greet us with a smile, they are sending us important information about their intentions. If we return the smile, we do the same. When our brains detect strangers who are different from us, a smile is the universal nonverbal cue that our intentions are friendly. Extensive research shows that smiling shifts the mindset of the person displaying it. When we greet people with an intentional smile, even when that may not be our initial predisposition, we are actually less likely to harbor prejudicial or suspicious thoughts about them.[4] When it comes to respect, both giving and receiving smiles are pretty important.

> The shortest distance between two people is a smile.
>
> Anonymous

One word of caution: if you are not the type of person who has developed the reputation for smiling, be patient with its impact on those around you, especially those you don't know well. The brain tends to become suspicious when it detects abnormal behavior patterns from people we already know. For example, if I were to go home and unexpectedly surprise my wife with flowers, I think her first response would be to ask me what I did or what I wanted. That notwithstanding, cultivating the habit of smiling when we meet people eventually pays considerable dividends to the quality of our relationships.

CHAPTER 8 # Changing Behavior Is the Key

A s powerful as the 12 rules of respect can be, it would be unfair to proceed without spending some time exploring the psychology and science of changing behavior. We've all failed at changing our behaviors at one time or another. Even when we've felt motivated to change the way we do things, old habits die hard. Whether we're talking about individuals or organizations, there are three essential ingredients required for successful and sustained behavior change.

The first of these is *awareness* that change is necessary in the first place. This can be a challenge in itself. If we're not aware that the way we're currently doing something isn't working or that there might be a better way, all bets are off. There is zero incentive to even try to change.

Let's assume that, for this discussion, we've had a burst of clarity and can see a better way. "I know that I would be perceived as being more respectful if I [fill in the blank]. I can also see how this would likely increase cooperation in our department." This still isn't enough. Assuming that we've reached this conclusion of our own free will, we then must develop a deep, personal *commitment* to adopt the new behavior. In some cases, this commitment may be individual, and in others it may be collective. Either way, it engages a part of our brains called the *limbic system*, which increases both our focus and motivation to take action on our intentions. Without this emotional valence, that "better way" is likely to remain an abstract notion that can easily be derailed by more pressing matters.

Keep in mind that fear can interrupt commitment to change. I was recently working with a new client in the financial services arena that, according to almost all senior leaders, desperately needed a cultural makeover. There were rampant and deep-seated behavioral challenges related to a lack of trust, unwillingness to hold each other accountable for outcomes, and an inability to make tough decisions. And this was with the leaders themselves. Imagine the tone this set for everyone else in the organization. Despite their recognition that the culture had become borderline dysfunctional (the company's poor financial performance laid to rest any doubts), several of the more tenured leaders were remarkably resistant to committing themselves to new behaviors. Even getting them to agree to support leadership training that specifically targeted the root causes of some of their issues required some serious arm twisting. The reason, as I discovered, had nothing to do with a lack of awareness of what they needed. It had to do with fear—fear that their personal efforts to change would be unsuccessful and fear that they would lose respect or even status as a result.

> People aren't afraid of change itself. They're afraid of the pain they might experience when they're not in control of change.

Even when we conquer our fears and develop resolve to change, there's one more ingredient we need before we change—the willingness to *practice* new behaviors until we become proficient at them. It is simply a matter of neural physiology. The behavior patterns we use the longest are the ones our brains are most skilled and efficient at using, even if they're not the ones we want. This includes our interaction styles and patterns with other people. If I was a good listener yesterday, I'll probably be a good listener today and again tomorrow. If I habitually yelled when I got angry in the past, I most likely will yell in the future. Either way, these are the pathways our brains have gotten very efficient at activating. Every time we activate an existing neural pathway, we make it even stronger.

The adult human brain weighs about four and a half pounds and is composed of approximately 100 billion neurons. Each of those neurons can be connected to 10,000 other neurons in an intricate network of synaptic pathways. Think of it as an extraordinarily complex map of roads and highways. Some of the connections are little more than dirt paths. Others are country roads, and the busiest ones are eight-lane super highways. The skills and behaviors we use most are executed through neural pathways that tend to be highly *myelinated*. Myelin is a substance made of fatty acids and protein that coats our frequently activated neural pathways and improves the efficiency and speed of electrical impulses moving through them. While we are able to "drive" on the country roads and dirt paths, the trip is slow, and we are likely to encounter detours. Our brains prefer to stick with tasks and behaviors that can be successfully performed with the least amount of effort.

A Simple Experiment

On a blank sheet of paper, sign your name somewhere in the middle of the page with either a pen or pencil. Pay attention to how easily your hand grabs the writing instrument and executes the task.

After you're done, position your pen a few inches above the original signature, close your eyes, and sign your name again. If you're like most people, you will be able to execute the task with the same ease and comfort as you did the first time. The finished product, your signature, probably looks almost identical to your original signature. What's interesting about this experiment is that it shows how efficiently our brain can execute a task even when it's deprived of its most dominant sensory input, vision.

continued

Now, switch your pen or pencil to your nondominant writing hand, keep your eyes open, and sign your name again directly below your original signature. Unless you're ambidextrous, you'll find this task far more difficult to complete even though your eyes are open. More importantly, the task will take longer to execute with poor results when compared to your standard signature. Did you notice the feedback your brain gave you when you forced yourself to execute a task in a manner that you were not efficient in? We typically experience a nagging urge to get back to the "right" way of doing things.

As simple as this experiment is, it demonstrates how powerful our current behavior patterns are in influencing how we will respond in the future. It also demonstrates the feedback that our brains generate when we are trying to change behavior. Performing tasks in a new way or training ourselves to respond differently to familiar situations takes more energy, in the form of glucose, for our brains to execute. The reason for this inefficiency is that the brain must create new neural pathways each time it completes a new or infrequently performed task.

With our brains having a bias toward sticking with existing neural pathways whenever possible, how do we change behaviors? How do we alter our interaction styles and the attitudinal orientations that drive our behaviors? The simple answer is to practice. When we practice something, especially when it's driven by motivation to improve, we get better. The trick is to stick with new behaviors long enough to enable the brain to become comfortable and proficient with them.

One of the most fascinating topics in the field of brain science is *neuroplasticity*, the brain's ability to create new physical pathways to support new skills and behaviors. It's encouraging to note that current research suggests that our brains can remain "plastic" for most people well into their eighties. Contrary to popular belief, old dogs can learn new tricks provided they want to learn them.

A Tool for Strengthening Our Capacity for Respect

When it comes to changing personal behavior, most of us fall into the category of *consciously incompetent*. That is to say, we know what we'd like to do (or not do), but we just have a hard time doing it, at least consistently. For those changes that are really important to us, how can we do a better job of rewiring our brains more effectively—reinforcing the desired neural pathways—so that the desired behaviors stick? Fortunately, neuroscience may now add the weight of hardcore brain research to theories first discussed in the mid-1800s, developed and refined in the late 1960s by sports psychologists, and almost continuously refined by mainstream psychology practitioners since.

In 1852, English physician and physiologist William Benjamin Carpenter first hypothesized that our actions and behaviors were not always conscious, but sometimes simply the by-products of what our brains were experiencing or perceiving about their environments (*automatic* or *reflex movements*).[1] Similarly, his pioneering work on the *adaptive unconscious* (which formed the foundation for today's modern field of cognitive psychology) led him to conclude that behaviors triggered unconsciously were not only faster and required less effort than those generated by conscious thought but also less prone to modification. It was precisely because of the strength and rigidity of these impulses that he believed our unconscious prejudices could be so dangerous and socially damaging. The question, then, was could our underlying thoughts and beliefs be changed, and, if so, how? For the majority of the next 100 years, the most direct approach that psychologists could offer was hypnosis—maybe.

Then in 1984, Colorado State University psychologist Richard Suinn suggested that a process he called *visual motor behavior rehearsal* (VMBR). This was a cognitive training technique to be used by athletes that would allow them perform more reliably under conditions of high-pressure competition.[2] The basic components of this approach focused on relaxation, building confidence, and using skill-specific (such as pitching or free-throw shooting) mental imagery with which the brain could practice. In theory, this would build robust thought patterns that the brain could automatically execute, even under the high pressure of athletic competition. It was only in the years since his original paper that neuroscientists figured out how the use of VMBR can result in actual physical changes to the brain that make improved performance more likely.

Using VMBR to Practice Respect

What does all this have to do with increasing our capacity for treating others with greater respect? If athletes can use mental imagery and practice to become better skiers, pole-vaulters, or archers, then you or I should also be able to use it to become a better listener, a more patient manager, or a more frequent giver of compliments. The mechanics are the same, and the impacts on the brain are similar. While the exact origins of the term are hard to nail down, the term *affirmation* is probably as close as we're going to get to the nonathletic equivalent of VMBR. A term that I like better, because of its descriptive power, is *affirmative reminder*. An affirmative reminder can be any collection of words, images, or other sensory inputs (or a combination of several) that triggers the brain to practice or mentally rehearse a specific action or mode of being (such as calm).

Interestingly, the entire practice of advertising is based on this very principle. When we're exposed to images that take us to a desired future state, both the pleasure and motivation centers in the brain are activated (see Figure 8.1). Specifically, the *nucleus accumbens* triggers the release of the neurotransmitter dopamine from the *ventral tegmental area* (VTA), which then is picked up by receptors back in the nucleus accumbens, the *amygdala*, the *septum*, and the *prefrontal cortex*. Working in concert with each other,

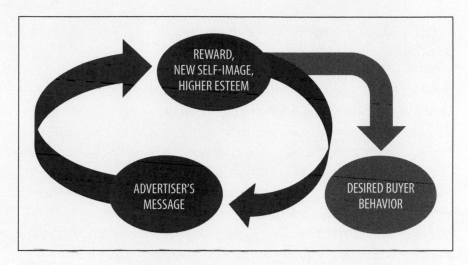

Figure 8.1   Traditional advertising model

these parts of the brain make up what is referred to as the brain's *pleasure circuit*. When properly activated, this mechanism encourages us to take action toward the desired future state. The next time you're watching television or come across an interesting print ad that catches your eye, pay attention to how your brain responds to the cues being presented. It can be as simple as seeing someone with tight abs and a toned waist exercising with the lasted fitness product. It could be the feeling of power or prestige evoked by watching someone drive a new luxury car. If the images and pleasure circuit activation are strong enough (which is what advertisers hope), then you will be moved toward buying the product or at least be nudged closer toward buying it.

What this means is that affirmative reminders are essentially self-directed advertising campaigns. By designing and exposing yourself to sensory experiences (words, pictures, smells, sounds, textures, etc.) that "reward" your brain for imagining itself performing certain actions or behaviors, you're doing two things. First, you're increasing your motivation to actually perform the desired behavior in the future. Second, you're actively practicing the behavior itself (albeit through your imagination) and actually getting better at it. This truly is where the power of your brain to rewire itself fully comes to the fore.

When reinforced through repetition, it's also where the similarity with commercial advertising continues. Every time you imagine yourself demonstrating a behavior with another person that makes you feel good (such as making direct eye contact, smiling, and paying a compliment), you're actively strengthening the same neural circuitry required for the demonstration of that behavior in real life (see Figure 8.2). If imagined with enough frequency, the desired behavior can actually become automatic or reflexive, as hypothesized by W.B. Carpenter over 150 years ago. More recently, Dr. Victor Pendleton offered the following perspective:

> *Every day we see these symbols scattered throughout our environment. In a similar manner, affirmative reminders are personally meaningful words or images that we use to remind ourselves of the behavior that we aspire to. We may use affirmative reminders to influence personal behavior of all kinds and to increase studying, healthy eating, generosity, and understanding.*[3]

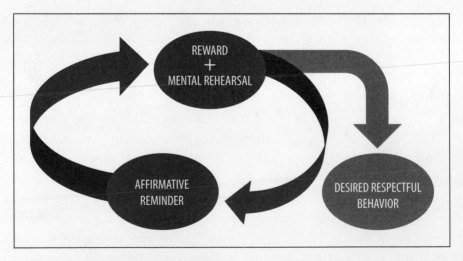

Figure 8.2   Affirmative reminder cycle

Affirmative reminders, when used consistently, give us the greatest tool possible for becoming not only more respectful, but more whatever we desire. They give us authorship to write the script for truly becoming our best selves. One of my favorite examples of the power of affirmative reminders involves a woman who attended one of our workshops through her employer, a county social services agency in Ohio. While always upbeat and polite on the outside, "Donna" struggled with her weight, her self-esteem, and her overall enthusiasm for life in general. She later confided, "Using affirmations sounded a bit hokey and too good to be true. After all, I'd been this way for many years. I was overweight, out of shape, and just kind of 'blah' about life. I tried to fake being happy, but then I just felt like a fraud. The worst part was, because I was unhappy with myself, I knew I wasn't giving my best effort to either my co-workers or our clients. I was just kind of going through the motions, day in and day out."

But to Donna, even the distant hope that affirmative reminders could possibly give her that extra nudge to break from her current reality made them worth trying. And try she did. Six months after the workshop, our facilitator went back to lead a follow-up session. Donna was in the class, but not as the old Donna. Thinking she was a new employee, our facilitator went to introduce himself to her before the session started. Donna just laughed. "Glen, she said with a big smile, "you know who I am. You just don't recognize me. But that's okay because I'm only half of who I used to be!"

The affirmative reminder process to create her own, personal advertising campaign was a catalyst for change unlike anything she had tried before. Not only had Donna transformed into the physical person she had only dreamed of being just months before, but her entire demeanor had changed. She had poise, energy, and a passion to help others that had been mostly hidden by over a decade of self-loathing and the feeling of helplessness. Evidently, others noticed the changes in Donna as well. Her rediscovered passion for not only helping the agency's clients, but also mentoring some of the newer employers had led to her being promoted to a manager's position earlier that month. She had truly become the author of her own future.

Selling Yourself on a More Respectful You

If you know how to do it, the process of designing your own advertising campaign with affirmative reminders is not only simple, but it's also immensely empowering. Imagine the confidence that you would begin to develop knowing that you could successfully and consistently develop new and change old behavioral habits (even some that are deeply ingrained). Applied toward the goal of creating a more respectful work environment, imagine the positive impact that you would have on the esteem, confidence, morale, and even performance of yourself and others within your organization.

The Groundwork

Like every good ad campaign, the most important work is done well before anyone ever sees or hears an ad spot. You first have to define your target market. That's you in this case. Then you have to find out what's important to that audience; what values you can connect with that are important to the audience and have long-term meaning. In this case, that means really knowing yourself, both as you are today and as you aspire to be tomorrow. Then you have to craft a message that will resonate with that desired future state so powerfully that it motivates you to take action. For you, this means knowing what your reward circuit hot buttons are and how to activate them so that they encourage behavior change. Accordingly, the preliminary steps for designing your own respect ad campaign are:

1. Create a short list (no more than five) of your top values that are compatible with (and maybe even strengthened by) respectful treatment of others. While your list will be unique to you, what's important is that the values be freely chosen (as opposed to being included out of guilt or a feeling that they *should* be on your list). Also, the values that you select should have the power to inspire you to take action. Finally, you know what they look like behaviorally to you (i.e., *collaboration*

could be demonstrated by taking turns talking or by asking a peer for his or her opinion). Here is a short list of potential values that others have shared:

- Family
- Fairness
- Loyalty
- Collaboration
- Helpfulness
- Harmony
- Intelligence
- Love
- Commitment
- Professional success
- Kindness
- Service to others
- Spontaneity
- Equality
- Creativity
- Freedom
- Romance
- Recognition
- Faith
- Integrity
- Health
- Fun
- Dignity
- Education
- Security
- Independence
- Spirituality
- Honesty
- Teamwork
- Compassion
- Adventure
- Wisdom
- Work-life balance
- Passion/energy
- Autonomy
- Discipline

2. Once you have your list of top values identified, challenge yourself to identify specific behaviors that would communicate respect to others and help you live in closer alignment with your personal values. Table 8.1 contains some examples.

   What you'll likely discover is that there are very few values that are incompatible with the demonstration of respect toward others. In fact, when we step back and look at the situation objectively, respectful treatment of others almost always makes it easier to live in alignment with whatever the our core values are.

Table 8.1   Linking Values with Respectful Behaviors

Value	Supporting respectful behavior
Intelligence	By making the time to solicit and listen to the ideas of others, I'm increasing my own awareness and intelligence.
Security	By making a conscious effort to look out for the well-being and safety of others, they will likely do the same for me.
Adventure	By taking the time to get to know new people when I travel, I gain a deeper sense of our similarities and differences.
Health	By forming deep, mutually rewarding friendships with people, I am contributing to our mutual physical and emotional health and well-being.
Fairness	By looking for opportunities to recognize my peers for their unique contributions to our success, I'm helping to create a work environment in which everyone feels important and valued.

3. The final step in building the foundation for your ad campaign is to figure out what your reward circuit hot buttons are. These would be any visual cues (pictures), sounds, smells, tastes, or even tactile triggers that cause the firing of your brain's reward circuits, thereby triggering the release of dopamine and encouraging your brain to take action. As with values, we each have a unique combination of sensory inputs that get our brains fired up and motivated to take action. Pictures are particularly powerful because they are processed by the brain's visual cortex, the most dominant of all its sensory processing centers. But particular sounds, smells, or even the feel of certain objects can also be powerful. Following are lists of possible mental cues volunteered by clients and associates:

PICTURES
- Significant other
- Your children or family
- Favorite place (beach, forest, desert, or mountain scene)
- Your work team or peer group

- Parents
- Historical or spiritual leader
- Any symbol or logo that has personal meaning

SOUNDS

- Recorded message from partner or child
- Clip from a favorite song
- Son or daughter practicing an instrument
- Waves or a running stream
- Kids laughing in a playground
- The voice of a parent talking
- Songbirds or nature sounds

SMELLS OR FRAGRANCES

- Cologne or perfume that reminds you of someone
- Vanilla, cinnamon, or other fragrant spices
- Suntan lotion or coconut oil
- Hot coffee
- Hot apple pie
- Freshly baked bread

The Message

Once the foundational elements have been thought through and organized, it's time to combine them into a powerful "ad" that serves as a positive basis of motivation for reinforcing specific behaviors. As with most commercial ads, the most important element is the script. The specific purpose of an affirmative reminder is twofold. First, it is to provide the emotional stimulus that will mobilize you to take some positive action. The second is to give our brains a crystal clear picture of what that action or behavior looks and feels like. The more precise and detailed the description, the clearer the picture and the easier it is for the brain to imagine and "practice" the behavior. Just like a muscle that is regularly flexed, each intentional rehearsal (even imagined) of a desired behavior strengthens the neural networks necessary for repeating the behavior in real life. According to Dr. Ellen Weber:

> *The brain changes as a function of where an individual focuses his or her attention. Every time I vent, I grow and link new brain cells for that purpose, and over time, I get better at it.*
>
> *But you can focus your attention on positive behavior and grow those connections as well. The brain can be wired for positive or toxic behavior. It's up to each individual to decide which will become more predominant.*[4]

There are many different approaches and guidelines to writing affirmations and affirmative reminders. In even a casual Internet search on the theme, you will find some common elements in most of them, like using "I" statements. You will also find some that conflict with each other. For example, some practitioners suggest that you keep them short; others that you make them long and descriptive. Some suggest that you keep them safe and comfortable. Others recommend that you challenge yourself and push beyond what you think is currently possible. My suggested approach is based on both the latest research in brain science and almost 20 years of client work and feedback. It consists of seven basic elements:

1. **Write from a first-person vantage point.** On this point, almost all practitioners agree. To be personally relevant, affirmative reminders must include the use of "I" rather than detached or hypothetical third persons.

> Incorrect: Great leaders and bosses look people in the eye when they talk with them.
>
> Correct: I look people in the eye when I speak with them.

Additionally, we want to articulate the experience not as if we were watching ourselves in a video, but rather as if it were unfolding in front of our own eyes. The next time you're watching TV, pay attention to the artful ways that advertisements try to simulate the actual driving experience that you would have in the vehicles being sold. It may be the smooth sound of a revving engine coupled with the driver's eye-view of racing though hairpin curves in a flashy, new sports coupe. Or it could be the sight of mud splashing up past the windshield as the driver bounces through a pothole pocked construction site in a beefy looking pickup truck.

What the ad agencies and their clients know is that this kind of first-person, virtual experience can feel enough like the real experience to trigger the reward circuits in our brains if we enjoy the experience they are creating for us. The hope, then, is that this causes us to take some positive "next step" toward purchasing, or at least test driving, their product. So why not use the same approach in the design of our affirmative reminders? As long as the experience we're describing is pleasurable, it will have a similar effect.

Incorrect: I see myself smiling and saying, "Good morning" to my coworkers.

Correct: I feel a smile spread across my face as I enter my office and warmly say, "Good morning" to my coworkers.

---

2. **Always write in the present tense.** Behavior change is all about, "Fake it 'til you make it." Although we're trying to trigger new behaviors in the future, we have to write about them as if they are in place now. While some practitioners feel that this may be perceived as "lying to ourselves" and potentially inhibit the desired change, what it really does is

create a positive form of cognitive dissonance. It creates a conflict for the brain (I'm not this way now), but does so with an option that is more attractive than the current reality. Again, the parallels with commercial advertising are striking.

> The greatest thing is, at any moment, to be willing to give up who we are in order to become all that we can be.
>
> Max de Pree, Businessman and Author

Writing affirmative reminders in the present instead of the future tense also does something else. It causes the brain to more reliably fire the associated neural pathway in the brain responsible for the physical behavior. Remember, the brain is wired for efficiency and may very well take a pass on exerting itself to activate a currently weak pathway if given the chance. Writing in the future tense makes it too easy for the brain to rationalize, "Okay, I will do this new behavior—eventually. But not right now. I've already got a lot going on today." Writing in the present tense eliminates this escape route.

> Incorrect: I will pay more attention to the suggestions of my subordinates.
>
> Correct: I pay close attention to the ideas and suggestions of my subordinates.

3. **Describe specific, desired behaviors and outcomes.**
The best-written affirmative reminders are effective, in part, because they describe an intended future behavior, action, or outcome so precisely that the brain has an easy road map

to follow for re-creating and practicing it. This means that we should be liberal with the use of adjectives and adverbs when describing the desired behavior. In some cases, it may be advantageous to use two or even three connected sentences.

Incorrect: I look for ways to compliment my subordinates and peers.

Correct: I am always on the lookout for new ways to recognize the contributions of my peers. When they stay late to complete assignments, I let them know how their efforts help the team. I also let them know how much I personally appreciate their commitment.

Along this same line of thinking, do your best to avoid stating your desired behaviors by what you want to avoid. For example, if you want to develop greater patience when dealing with others who push your buttons, you might think it would be reasonable to write something along the lines of, "I do not lose my temper when …" The problem with this is that our brains immediately focus on and translate the action words (*lose my temper*) into pictures of the behavior that you're actually trying to avoid. Then the brain fires the neural pathway that you're trying to change and not the new one. So stick with words that describe the actual desired behavior.

Incorrect: I do not criticize people who do not share my beliefs.

Correct: I listen with an open mind to people whose experiences and perspectives are different from mine.

4. **Make it aspirational by using language that connects to your values.** The best-written affirmative reminders are effective because they create two types of road maps for the brain: a behavioral one and an emotional one. Using language that links our affirmative reminders to our aspirations to live in closer alignment with our core personal values can be a powerful and durable source of motivation. Specifically, it supports the sensory triggers (more on that later) that engage both the reward circuits and other regions within the brain's limbic system. Over time, the continued activation of these circuits builds emotional impetus and creates a sort of *neural gravity* that literally pulls us toward the new behavior.

   This element is critical for another reason as well. It helps to minimize the potential for the type of cognitive dissonance that could derail our change efforts. If there is a conflict between the described new behavior and what our brains associate with being in our best interest, then the "ad" fails to register. It would be akin to what would happen in the brain of a vegetarian watching an advertisement for a steak house. Either nothing registers at all or, worse, the viewer is actually repulsed by the message.

   More related to respectful behaviors, a real conflict could arise around the new behavior of "helping others more." While one part of my brain sees it as a good thing, another may worry that it will mean more work for me (which may be the reason we're not doing this already). By specifically mapping out the connection between the new behavior and believable, value-aligned benefits back to ourselves, we minimize the likelihood of this conflict.

Incorrect: I look for ways to compliment my subordinates and peers.

> Correct: I am always on the lookout for ways to recognize the contributions of my peers. By letting them know how their efforts make a difference, it promotes camaraderie and esteem, and helps us hit our performance targets.

5. **Use descriptive language that details context or environment.** Similar to a previous step, the more details you can add about when and where your desired behaviors should be demonstrated, the better the road map you create for your brain. Challenge yourself to come up with descriptions that capture your desired mindset, nonverbal cues, specific meetings/routines, places, times of the day, or even specific individuals.

> Incorrect: I ask others what they think.
>
> Correct: When in staff meetings, I make it a point to demonstrate a friendly, curious disposition with Bill, Liz, and Connie as I invite them to share their opinions and ideas. I then show my true appreciation for their input by giving them my thoughtful, undivided attention when they speak.

6. **Use "learning curve" language and avoid absolutes.** Rome wasn't built in a day and behavior change doesn't happen overnight. It's a process of gradual shifts in our default modes of both interacting with others and responding to cues in our environment. The neural pathways that house old behavior patterns can hang around for quite a while, which means that we're always prone to have occasional setbacks. I really try to be more patient, but sometimes (especially when

I'm stressed) I may fly off the handle. Because of this, we want to avoid using affirmative reminder language that can box us in and make us feel like a failure when we don't act at our best. Avoid using words like "always," "never," and "every time" because they are absolute and can potentially trigger negative self-talk and feedback when we're not perfect. Instead, use modifiers like "more and more," "consistently," and "try my best." While still moving us forward, these phrases take into consideration that we're not perfect and allow us to get back on track quickly after setbacks.

> Incorrect: I always say "Good morning" to my coworkers when I start a new workday.
>
> Correct: More and more, I start my workdays on a positive note by greeting my co-workers by name with a friendly "Good morning."

7. **Keep the process upbeat and fun.** Affirmative reminders work only when we look forward to reviewing them (the next step). As a final "lens" to look through while writing them, make sure that the overall tone that you're setting is positive, upbeat, inspiring, and even fun. Be on guard against wording that triggers guilt, drudgery, or a burden.

> Incorrect: I make time to listen to others because it's what a good manager should do.
>
> Correct: I look forward to taking time each morning to meet with and explore the ideas of my subordinates. Not only does it esteem them, but it's a great way to start the day and it makes me better informed when forming my own opinions.

The Final Product

Adding all these elements together is as much of an art as it is a skill. We all have different writing styles and vocabularies. Some of us are more comfortable capturing our thoughts with words. On top of that, some behaviors are easier to put into words than others (giving compliments versus being empathetic). After almost 20 years, I still pick up tips and suggestions from seminar participants during almost every workshop. While certainly not perfect, here are a few examples of some fairly well-crafted affirmative reminders (see the Appendix for a more comprehensive list of examples):

- More and more, I look forward to taking small breaks throughout the day to sit and talk with my employees about things that are important to them. Whether their concerns are personal or business related, letting them know that I see them as people first reminds me that we're all on similar journeys.
- With a smile on my face and pen in hand, I look forward to writing personal thank-you notes to our clients each Friday. It gives me a tremendous sense of pride knowing that I've helped win their confidence as a valued business partner, and sharing that appreciation with them further builds our relationship.
- I am only one person, but even by myself, I am powerful enough to make a difference in the quality of other people's lives. I consistently make the time do small things, like clean up after myself (and even after others when time permits). Whether it's the office or my neighborhood, my goal is to leave our shared spaces attractive and beautiful for everyone to enjoy.

An Alternative Approach

There is recent research suggesting that there may be more than one way to design an effective affirmative reminder. Thus far, I have described what is referred to as the declarative self-talk approach. In 2010,

continued

researchers at the University of Illinois and University of Southern Mississippi concluded that an interrogative approach of self-talk may be even more powerful[5]. While the experiments used by the researchers used a much simpler sentence structure than we have proposed (*"I will"* vs. *"Will I?"* priming statements), the results were fairly uniform. When preceded by a question instead of a statement, the researchers' sample groups performed the studied tasks better.

Although a fairly significant departure from the traditional approach to designing affirmative reminders, an interrogative approach makes perfect sense when you think about generating specific images in the brain. A question such as *"How will I demonstrate respect during our staff meeting?"* causes the brain to focus on very specific behaviors that could satisfy this goal. This artificial creation of a problem to be solved (vs. a behavior to be imagined) may actually increase the total amount of focus that the brain brings to bare on the effort. One caveat that should be stated here is that alignment with our values is crucial for this approach to be effective. "How will I be more supportive of my peers?" will not be as effective if the related behaviors are only weakly connected to my core values or outcomes that are not perceived to be particularly important to me.

The Campaign

Now that your affirmative reminders have been written, the next step is to combine them with the previously discussed sensory cues (pictures, sounds, etc.) and then put a plan in place for practicing them. Let's start with the combining the elements first. The goal here is to create a "commercial" for your brain that, when played, creates immediate emotional reward and then provides a behavioral instruction set that prompts you to imagine yourself demonstrating the precise behavior with as much detail as possible. The best way to do this is to prime with a reward circuit trigger first and then deliver the message. To use a farming metaphor, think of it as tilling a field before you plant the seeds. By priming your brain with a pleasurable experience first (tilling the soil), you make it easier for the behavioral patterns that you're trying to reinforce through your affirmative reminders (the seeds) to activate the corresponding neural pathways and get stronger (take root). Just as importantly, you're increasing the desire and sense of urgency to demonstrate the behaviors in real life (adding fertilizer).

The most common approach to combining these elements requires nothing more than paper, pen, scissors, and Scotch tape. When I was first introduced to a basic version of the process by former colleagues at Edge Learning Institute, we would simply advise our workshop participants to write the affirmative reminders by themselves on 3 by 5 index cards. The problem with this was that black ink on a white index card by itself didn't work for everyone (including me). Even if they were good at writing and could capture their behaviors and emotions with words well, many people would lose interest in the process because the emotional drive to follow through just wasn't strong enough.

What solved this challenge for many participants almost immediately was the addition of visual cues. We asked them to find pictures that captured their attention, were personally meaningful, and were associated with strong, positive emotional memories. With scissors and tape in hand, we began clipping and taping pictures of our children, spouses, favorite vacations, nature scenes, and even favorably remembered work events with colleagues all around the perimeter of the words on the index cards. (See Figure 8.3.) Because the natural tendency is for our eyes to look at the pictures first, the images were priming our reward circuits with all kinds of feel-good emotions prior to even reading the actual affirmative reminders. It worked like a charm!

With technology improving almost yearly, some people got even more creative. They began to use word processing or desktop publishing software to electronically combine the elements and add background colors and fancy fonts. Some turned their more important affirmative reminders into small posters or background images on their computer screens.

More and more, I exhale, smile, and relax as I realize that the key to success is balance. There is plenty of time for work, ample time for family and play, and sufficient time for health, relaxation, and sleep.

Figure 8.3   Sample affirmative reminder card

Using All Our Senses to Help Us Change

My daughter Olivia shares the credit for one of the more ingenious augmentations to the process—the addition of our olfactory senses. One day, when she was five years old, she walked into my home office as I was working on a personal affirmative reminder for relaxation. With a mischievous grin, she held up her little hand and said, *"Daddy, smell my finger!"* My brain quickly assessed all likely possibilities (and factored in her known delight in tricking me), and decided that I needed more information.

"Now why should I do that?" I asked, smiling with feigned distrust.

She giggled and said, "Just do it. I promise you'll like it!"

Call me crazy, but I threw caution to the wind, leaned over, and went for it. She was right; I did like it. She had been helping my wife pack for our upcoming vacation to Florida and found the suntan lotion. That's what was on her finger. The intoxicating aroma of coconut oil (and whatever else the folks at Banana Boat put in that stuff to make it smell so good) was potent! It immediately brought a smile to my face, relaxed my body, and transported my mind to a towel-covered chaise lounge on my favorite beach, complete with the sounds of seagulls and ocean waves. Not only was I pleasantly surprised, but the experience triggered a "Eureka!" moment for me. What if we added the power of scent to visual cues in order to strengthen the affirmative reminder process?

As it turns out, our sense of smell is controlled by the brain's olfactory circuit, which is also part of the limbic system (tied to our emotions). While not as sensitive in humans as in other mammals, what makes this system such a potentially powerful tool to help reinforce new behaviors is that it is remarkably quick and tied directly to our long-term memory. The smell of something that is linked to past experiences, people, or accomplishments for which we have strong, favorable memories can be very powerful. It can almost immediately trigger the pleasure circuit emotions needed to help encourage our brains to imagine a new behavior that is somehow related. It should come as no surprise that I immediately smeared a little suntan oil on the back of my affirmative reminder supporting relaxation. The affirmation sequence then became (1) smell the suntan oil, (2) look at the picture (of my own feet propped up in front of the ocean), and (3) read the affirmative reminder.

Obviously, if you can use the power of smell, you could conceivably use any of the five senses to create the right emotional backdrop. Favorite songs, voices, or other sounds can trigger memories. So can certain tastes and even holding certain objects, like a medal or favorite scarf that belonged to a parent. What's important is how you combine and sequence all these reward inputs with your affirmative reminders to create a powerful ad campaign for change. Based on the farming model described earlier, the best approach is to:

1. Expose yourself to the reward circuit primers for a few seconds
2. Settle into the emotional zone that allows you to relax and focus

3. Read the affirmative reminder slowly, allowing your brain to vividly imagine yourself demonstrating the desired behavior(s) and background elements

Helpful hint: Rather than reading them silently, some people like to record themselves reading their affirmative reminders and then play the recordings back. For some people, it appears that the actual sound of their own voice stating the desired behavior out loud improves the imprinting process in their brains.

Running Your Respect Ad Campaign

Although you may be good at creating effective messages, every competent advertising executive knows something else about running an effective campaign. No matter how compelling the message, if it's played only once or twice, there's very little chance of it influencing perceptions and intentions strongly enough to result in the desired buyer behaviors. The same holds true with your affirmative reminder campaign. To work, the process requires repetition, repetition, repetition! It's not that your brain doesn't "get it" after the first exposure. It does. After all, you wrote the message. But unlike a computer, which can immediately execute new software updates once they're installed, the synaptic pathways that govern our automatic behaviors (remember W. B. Carpenter?) are much more durable and resistant to quick fixes or change. They require a slow, steady, and consistent prompting to practice the new behavioral "code" so that the required synaptic myelination can occur and that the new behaviors eventually become almost effortless. Remember how it felt to sign your name with your nondominant hand? It was awkward, slow, required great concentration, and, for most of us, felt uncomfortable. But with repetition and practice, any one of us could learn to execute that task quickly, neatly, and with very little effort. We could do the same with almost any other behavior or skill (like being more patient around certain people) because the learning process that enables the brain to develop them is similar.

The final piece of the respect ad campaign puzzle is to create a schedule for rehearsing and practicing your affirmative reminders. While research and opinions on ideal frequency are all over the map, here are some general guidelines you can start with:

1. **Focus your efforts.** Start with no more than two to four affirmative reminders. While there's no reason that you couldn't eventually do more, give yourself a chance to develop proficiency with a few that are really important to you.

2. **Three to five times each day.** Try to identify at least three to five times throughout each day when you can comfortably put other priorities aside, relax, and dedicate a minute or two for "advertising" the more respectful you to yourself. At most, the total time commitment will be no more than 10 minutes each day.

3. **Schedule your ads in "prime time."** Pick the times for you that make sense from the perspective of there being the fewest distractions (beginning or end of day, lunchtime, etc.) and at events that may be where you want to ideally demonstrate the behaviors. For example, if you have a regularly scheduled staff meeting on Tuesday mornings, maybe take a few minutes right beforehand to mentally rehearse any reminders that would potentially be desirable in that setting (patience, listening, compliments, etc.).

4. **Put your schedule on the calendar.** Over the years, I've seen some wonderfully designed affirmative reminders written by both peers and workshop participants. Unfortunately, not all of them saw the light of day more than a few times. Until you actually get into a solid routine of reviewing your ads without prompting, put reminders on your daily schedules or calendar. With the advent of

smartphones that synchronize with our work computers, it's easier than ever to make sure you don't get too busy and forget to watch your personal ad channel.

5. **Include multiple environments.** While this book was written primarily with workplaces in mind, respect can be practiced in all the domains in which we spend time. Balance is important, so challenge yourself to come up with at least one affirmative reminder for reinforcing a new respectful behavior either at home, school, or in your social groups.

6. **Concentrate on proper form.** Just like practicing free throws in basketball or proper breathing while swimming laps, form counts. When your read (or listen to) your affirmative reminders, really focus on pushing your brain to imagine itself practicing the desired behavior as seen through your own eyes. The more you practice, the more comfortable, natural, and fluid the effort becomes.

Leveraging Technology for Your Ad Campaign

The use of word processing and desktop publishing software has made it easier than ever to create graphically rich, emotionally inspiring affirmative reminders. As effective as this is already, newer technology is now putting the power of self-directed behavior change literally at our fingertips. Even the most basic smartphones now allow us to do much more. We can put reminders to review our ad campaign on our mobile calendars. We can even put the ads themselves, with pictures, on our smart devices. As of late 2012, there were already over a dozen iPhone and Android apps offering basic platforms for designing and practicing affirmations and affirmative reminders. Even newer versions that offer the ability to integrate personal pictures, voices, and music are planned for release in the near future. For the very latest on this technology, visit www.LegacyCultures.com/myLegacy.

A Self-Sustaining Cycle

At some point, the imagined new behavior starts to feel so natural, that it begins to show up more and more frequently in our real life. Our confidence in our ability to positively change behaviors increases, and we develop an growing sense of efficacy (to be discussed more a bit later). Here is where another powerful force also begins to kick in. It's the power of positive feedback. Known as the father of *operant conditioning*, psychologist B. F. Skinner was able to demonstrate in 1948 that animals (including humans) are more likely to repeat a certain action or behavior when it is rewarded with *positive operants* or *reinforcers*. While future behavior can be influenced by *negative operants* or *punishers* as well, they're not as powerful or durable as the reinforcers.

When we treat people in a manner that they unambiguously interpret as being respectful toward them, they tend to respond favorably toward us in return. They smile, stand a little taller, maybe say thank you, or give some other subtle indication that they appreciated what we did. This makes us feel good. Just like with a basketball player who successfully sinks a winning free throw, this positive feedback that our practice has paid off triggers our brains' reward circuits. We then link these good feelings directly back to the behaviors, and the likelihood of our repeating them in the future goes up even more. The affirmative reminder process permits even a single person with enough commitment to start a cascade of change that spreads gradually but predictably to others. (See Figure 8.4.) Respectful behaviors feed on themselves and beget more respectful behaviors.

Be Patient with Yourself

One final point to keep in mind when you're trying to develop new behavior patterns: there will be times when we revert back to our

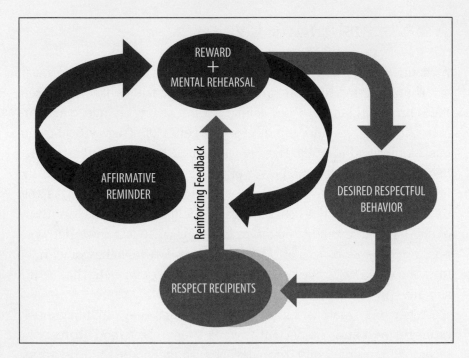

Figure 8.4   Affirmative reminder cycle with social reinforcement

old ways, particularly when we're under stress. Affirmative reminders help create new behavior patterns, but what about the old ones?
Even when it seems that we've turned the corner on the behaviors
that got in our way in the past, we will sometimes see the remnants
of our less flattering patterns emerge. My close friend and colleague
Dr. Paul Marciano puts it this way: "Behaviors that change too
quickly tend to change back quickly." Sometimes, we're just human.

When we occasionally relapse and display behaviors that we
know are disrespectful, the best thing to do is quickly apologize if
we offended someone, and try to practice the desired behavior and
bring the affirmative reminders back out for reinforcement. While
some old pathways may never be fully replaced, we can redirect
most of the future "traffic" to the desired pathways. Then, like infrequently traveled paths, the old neural pathways that go unexercised
for longer periods of time begin to "grow over" and eventually fade

away. Referred to as *pruning* by scientists, the ever-efficient brain rids itself of old pathways that are no longer required.

Respect Yourself in Order to Better Respect Others

If we want to bring our best selves into our interactions with others on a consistent basis, then the place to start for most of us is with ourselves. Taking care of ourselves physically, mentally, and emotionally makes it more likely that our best selves will be available to others. Even if we are a person who normally treats others with respect, we've all probably had one of those days when our interaction skills were lacking. We cut people off, jump to premature conclusions about their intentions, deliver an uncharacteristically sarcastic comment, or roll our eyes in exasperation. Physical energy, stress, and how we feel about ourselves all play a significant role in determining our capacity for treating others with respect. Let's now take a look at these elements more closely.

CHAPTER 9 Self-Esteem: The Art of Respecting Ourselves

Almost 20 years ago, I attended a personal development workshop where the concept of self-esteem was introduced. Even though I'd heard of it before, I had never had the subject thoroughly explained or linked to behavior and performance. The introduction of this subject illuminated for me what I believe to be one of people's greatest blind spots. Healthy self-esteem is not only a reliable predictor of a person's overall mental health and wellness but also of how that person treats others. It is almost impossible to treat other people with respect on a consistent basis unless we respect ourselves first.

Before we define self-esteem, let's make sure we know what it isn't. Over the years, there have been many people who have tried to downplay its importance and desirability by linking it to negative attributes such as egotism, arrogance, conceit, or a sense of predominance over others. These attitudes, and their related behaviors are far from those correctly linked to self-esteem and may actually be indicators of its absence. Because self-esteem is generally thought to have cognitive, affective, and behavioral manifestations, let's define it as follows:

> *Self-esteem is the degree to which individuals feel comfortable with themselves as they are, believe that they have inherent value as individuals, and demonstrate confidence in their ability to successfully achieve their own measure of success.*

People with healthy self-esteem can be characterized as those who have an intrinsic feeling of warm regard for themselves accompanied by a confidence in their ability to successfully navigate their world daily. The adjective *healthy* is intentional in this definition because it suggests a measure of self that is formed not in isolation, but with consideration for others around us. In contrast, there has been research that has linked the condition of *high* self-esteem to attitudes and behaviors such as conceit, bragging, bullying, or exploiting others.[1] These are socially undesirable qualities that can damage the productivity of coworkers and the organization overall.

What makes healthy self-esteem so important to our pursuit of respectful treatment of others is that it frees up valuable energy for building mutually healthy relationships. When people already have a strong emotional core, they expend a relatively small amount of time and effort nurturing their own ego. Because of this, they have more energy available to monitor and support the emotional well-being of those with whom they interact. Even if I value respect for others as a principle, a deficit with my own sense of worth can interfere with my ability to act accordingly.

Healthy self-esteem supports a broad range of attitudes and behaviors that are individually and organizationally beneficial. A few of these include:

- Assuming greater personal accountability for outcomes
- Building and maintaining healthier one-on-one relationships
- Being more receptive to new ideas and other people's approaches

- Demonstrating a greater capacity for empathy
- Comfortably and respectfully interacting with people who have different backgrounds and values
- Respectfully sharing opinions that may run counter to those of the majority
- Demonstrating socially appropriate levels of assertiveness
- Constructively managing criticism and feedback from others
- Proactively pursuing meaningful goals
- Regularly acknowledging and complimenting the contributions of others

In stark contrast, individuals with unhealthy self-esteem are more prone to perceptions, attitudes, and behaviors that hinder their performance and often harm others. They may act in ways that reflect their own low sense of worth in the following ways:

- Accepting poor treatment from others
- Talking disparagingly about themselves or their abilities
- Perpetually waiting for others to tell them what to do
- Demonstrating an excessive need for approval from others
- Greater susceptibility to being talked into decisions or behaviors that would otherwise go against their own values
- Reluctance to share their original ideas or thoughts out of fear of being judged unfavorably by others
- Stated pessimism about their expectations of future success and happiness

Depending on their personality, low self-esteem can also trigger more aggressive behaviors that reflect attempts to make people feel superior to others. These often include:

- Propensity to show off or boast about their accomplishments
- Bullying weaker personalities
- Publicly attacking or criticizing others who are viewed as threats
- Gossiping about others in ways that damage their reputation

- Passive-aggressive interaction styles
- Unwillingness to be wrong about most topics
- Pattern of hostility toward members of groups that they perceive as different
- Unwillingness to accept feedback on their behaviors from others

Future Interrupted

"Nancy" was, by all accounts, a "high-potential" employee for a Cincinnati, Ohio-based nonprofit healthcare provider. As a midlevel marketing manager, she had just walked out of her one-year performance review and could not have been happier. Based on both his own feedback and that of her peers, her boss "Henry" had given her an "exceeds requirements" on literally every measure possible. She was enthusiastic about her job, felt that her efforts were helping to actually make a difference, and had every reason to believe that she would continue to be successful for quite some time.

Later that day, it seemed that Nancy's accomplishments were being acknowledged when she was asked to participate in a marketing update meeting with a subcommittee of the organization's board of directors. In addition to Nancy and the board members, the meeting would be also be attended by both Henry and "Alice", the organization's CEO. While she had interacted briefly with the board members in the past, she was thrilled with the opportunity to share her observations and insights about the current marketing direction and felt confident in her ability to make a good impression for her team.

The meeting itself went exactly as Nancy had hoped. After presenting her overview of the organization's current marketing strategy and efforts, the board members thanked her and probed for more. Specifically, they wanted her candid perceptions of what could be done to improve the number of patient referrals into their facilities more quickly. Demonstrating a keen awareness of both the organization's current procedures and how they could be improved, Nancy was articulate, confident, and compelling in her recommendations, or so she thought.

The first sign of trouble came within an hour of the meeting's conclusion. While the board members were pleased and impressed with Nancy's insights and recommendations, Alice, it appeared, was not. In fact, word got back to Nancy through another meeting participant that Alice was enraged because she felt that Nancy had "over-volunteered" information and perceptions about some of the organization's internal practices that were actually hampering efforts to grow their outreach and client base. These perceptions, Alice reportedly felt, reflected poorly on her leadership and would result in the board members asking pointed questions of her. Nancy was as mortified by this revelation as she was surprised. Everything she had shared was done in good faith and in the spirit of helping to help drive improvement. More importantly, neither Alice nor Henry had ever coached her ahead of time on topics to avoid or details that were not to be shared at these meetings. She did the only thing she could think of, which was send Alice a heartfelt apology by e-mail for apparently overstepping her bounds. This message included a request for Alice's personal guidance so that Nancy could get a better grasp of the nuanced board communication expectations going forward. There was no reply to her message.

The following morning, Nancy was called in to meet with Alice and Henry to discuss the situation. Evidently the e-mail apology had not made much of a difference because Alice, while starting calmly, quickly digressed into a full-blown tirade. Attacking Nancy for "making the rest of us look like fumbling idiots," Alice at one point openly mocked Nancy in front of her boss, Henry. "I'm Nancy and, even though I've only been here for a year," she sneered, "this is what we're doing wrong, and here's what I think we should do!"

Recalling the situation later that day, Nancy reflected that the attack was so painful that she literally went numb. "It was like I was sitting there, but watching myself from the outside. I know I was there and was probably apologizing again, but don't really remember exactly what I said.

continued

Emotionally, I just sort of shut down and absorbed whatever she was saying. I felt completely helpless."

Very predictably, this marked the beginning of the end for this employee who was once thought to have high potential. Feeling that whatever goodwill she had earned was permanently destroyed, Nancy turned in her resignation two weeks later to pursue another opportunity. During both that time and her subsequent 30-day transition window, Alice never once apologized nor, for that matter, even spoke directly to her. There was just an awkward silence whenever the two passed in the hall or were in the same space. Even in the elevator on her very last day with the organization, nothing but aloofness—and more silence.

Ironically, the organization was forward-thinking enough to conduct exit interviews with employees who left voluntarily. But when Nancy shared the experience with the interviewing HR representative as the reason for her leaving, the response was, "I'm not surprised. In fact, we have several employees who won't even donate to our organization because of her." Since then, the organization has struggled as several talented individuals have either retired or left to pursue new opportunities. Alice the CEO remains.

A Rising Tide Lifts All Boats

Healthy self-esteem at the individual level promotes productive behaviors that can be contagious. Imagine for a moment that your coworkers showed up tomorrow with a slight boost in their level of self-esteem. They feel friendly, engaged, and have more confidence in their own knowledge, perceptions, and abilities. The effect would be like that of a rising tide in a harbor with many boats. All the boats sit higher, and because of the connectivity that exists between us, something else changes. They aren't just sitting higher in the water; they resonate around each other at a higher, happier, and more productive frequency. Given the obvious and observable impact of productivity, how can we get to this place?

Think of healthy self-esteem as a piggy bank that is almost full and the bank's owner as the primary beneficiary. This analogy is appropriate for two reasons. First, the person who owns the bank is responsible for its balance. Because having healthy self-esteem is a way we think and feel about ourselves, no one else has greater control. Second, other people can influence our esteem balance based on how they engage us. Remember the backpack analogy? If they treat us with respect, they can put a few extra coins into our bank. If they treat us with disrespect, they can take a few out.

Assuming that we are the primary guardians of our own esteem, how can we actively work on building and maintaining a healthy balance? The answer lies in a combination of increasing personal awareness, changing some of the stories we tell ourselves, and reevaluating some of the permissions that we give others. In all cases, the primary power and responsibility for improving the way we feel about ourselves resides with us. Let's take a closer look at some specific techniques we can use in this process.

Eight Steps for Building Respect for Ourselves

Following are eight steps we can follow to help us build our self-esteem.

1. Identify the Qualities and Skills That Are Most Closely Linked to Your Idea of Success

Current research on self-esteem is conclusive about one point: Self-esteem is linked to our sense of competence in the areas that are important to us. Specifically, it is linked to our individual perception of success and how well we're performing in its pursuit. For example, if my personal picture of success includes being physically fit, how I feel about myself will be a partial reflection of how I'm doing in this area. Minimally, it will be a reflection of my confidence in whether I believe I can make satisfactory progress in pursuit of my goals.

The most important consideration in this step is to double-check that our definitions of success are our own. We live in a world where people are constantly bombarded with manufactured and polished images of how we should look, dress, socialize, play, and even make love (cue the erectile dysfunction commercials with waterfalls, coy smiles, and bathtubs on the beach at sunset). If we base our image of success on the ideas offered by pop culture or the media, we risk pinning our emotional well-being to forever-changing illusions that are commonly out of our reach. Turn off the noise and tune into yourself. As you look at your current trajectory in life, what is the definition of success that gives you pride and passion in its pursuit?

2. Identify Your Current Strengths and Establish Plans for Improving Your Opportunity Areas

> You have to put in many, many, many tiny efforts that nobody sees or appreciates before you achieve anything worthwhile.
>
> Brian Tracy, Author, Keynote Speaker

Once you have clarified your personal definition of success, examine where you currently are relative to where you want to be. Figure out what you need to do to make positive adjustments and, as an old friend used to say, "Get after it!" Get off the sofa and get in shape. Spend more quality time with your spouse and your kids. Change your spending habits and start saving. Grab a laptop and start writing that book. Or jump on Expedia and look for island resorts that have double-wide bathtubs on a beach. Whatever your goals, there are few things more esteeming than knowing you're making progress toward the goals that match your picture of success.

3. Be on the Lookout for New Opportunities to Grow Your Talents and Experiences

Growth facilitates vitality and viability. Part of our sense of self-worth comes from the belief and confidence that we have the ability to be successful both today and in the future. Unfortunately, the skills, knowledge, and experiences that got us to our current position may not be enough to generate the results or accomplishment tomorrow. We inoculate ourselves against irrelevance by learning anything and everything we can. With a sense of adventure driven by curiosity, make it a point to try one or two new things each month that excite you and maybe a few that even scare you!

4. Identify and Redirect Unhealthy Competition and Comparisons

If there was one thing I wish my parents had drilled into me more intensely, it is to compete not with others, but with myself. Like many, I remember going through grade school and high school trying to keep up with the accomplishments of those around me. Intensified by the competitive nature of an all-male high school, I compared myself to others in everything—athletic prowess, academics, social popularity, and, of course, dating. While this may have contributed to me becoming fairly proficient at academics and sports, it came at a steep price. My sense of worth was often determined by my view of how well others did. Their accomplishments were sometimes simply more reasons for me to be unhappy with myself.

Foolish as it seems in retrospect, many adults continue to go through life this way, only the environmental props are different. In the back of their minds, they compare, in relation to their own situation, what they think other people earn and the kind of houses they live in, where they vacation, and what cars they drive. They look at what shoes someone wore to the party, who they hang out with, and who has the reputation for coming up with the wittiest remarks. They notice who got promoted ahead of them and whose idea got the most support at the last staff meeting. As personal finance guru Suze Orman so famously said, "Stop the madness!"

If you look at the unique mix of talent, skills, and knowledge each person possesses, no two people are alike. Why, then, would we want to judge ourselves against the accomplishments of others who are fundamentally different from us? Competition drives an invisible wedge between people. It sabotages teamwork and leaves feelings of isolation and alienation. In relation to self-esteem, competition with others hinders control of your own sense of worth. Their failures or shortcomings are your success, and their achievements are your pangs of inadequacy.

It is fine to notice what others accomplish. We are human, and that's part of how we determine how we fit in our world. Rather than feeling envy when others are successful, applaud them and, if appropriate, use them as inspiration. Don't forget that their "best" in any particular arena is just that— their best. If you compete with your own best at whatever you do, it is guaranteed that two things will happen. First, you'll fall asleep at night knowing you played the game of life to the best of your abilities that day. Second, tomorrow's best may well be even better.

5. Forgive Yourself for Past Mistakes and Poor Decisions

Having been raised Catholic and then marrying into a Jewish family, there was one constant I have been able to rely upon over the years: guilt. After almost 50 years, I feel certain in saying that, along with its cousin, regret, it is a thoroughly nonproductive emotion on which to dwell. While guilt can have a positive impact when it causes us to change or apologize for hurtful behaviors, too many people allow themselves to be held hostage by the mistakes they made weeks, months, and even years ago.

From a rational point of view, berating ourselves for past mistakes makes no sense. Whatever we did in the past is in the rearview mirror and can't be undone. Even though it now appears to have been the wrong decision, we believed it was the right thing to do at the time. That's because we complete a level of analysis, quick as it may be, prior to making decisions. Decision making is a complex process, and sometimes we don't place the correct weight on the right variables. Other times, we don't have all the data available that can lead to better decisions. Finally, sometimes we simply miscalculate the impact of our actions. The point is that we're human so we need to give ourselves a break on those occasions when we get it wrong.

> I am not discouraged, because every wrong attempt discarded is another step forward.
>
> Thomas Edison, American Inventor and Businessman

Being willing and able to forgive yourself for past mistakes accomplishes two important things. First, it frees up amazing amounts of energy that can be spent on current, more productive activities. Second, it breaks the cycle of synaptic reinforcement that reliving past mistakes perpetuates. When we continually replay memories of decisions or behaviors that we now regret, we ironically may be adding more myelin to the neural circuitry that was responsible for the inappropriate actions in the first place. Letting go and moving on is always a more beneficial course of action for all parties involved.

6. Hold Yourself Completely Accountable for Your Actions, Decisions, and Outcomes

Is there a legitimate place for short-term guilt and remorse? Yes. As previously mentioned, they are emotional indicators of discomfort that we internally generate when we sense that our decisions and behaviors were inappropriate or hurtful or that fell short of our own or others' expectations. For guilt to have a positive value, it must lead to some type of behavior change or related correction. If we make a mistake, we need to fix it to the best of our ability. If we complete a project improperly, we go back and do it the way it should have been done. If we damage a relationship, an apology is necessary given in the same venue in which the harm was done. When we consistently improve our personal accountability, it increases our overall sense of effectiveness and competence.

If you are a leader, manager, or supervisor, it is critical that you enforce a consistent policy of accountability for everyone who reports to you. If we excuse people who exhibit poor behaviors, disrespectful actions, or substandard work, it generates a lot of damage. Besides what it communicates to others within the organization, failing to hold people accountable may send subtle messages that damage an employee's self-esteem. It may be interpreted as, "I don't think you can do any better, so I'll accept what is and not expect more." Alternatively, it could signify, "What you were working on isn't that important, so it doesn't matter if you get it right." While ignoring poor behavior or performance may alleviate the potential for short-term conflict, it doesn't promote lasting confidence or competence.

7. Develop a Pattern of Self-Talk That Validates Your Worth and Abilities

Each of us has developed a particular way of interpreting and explaining the world around us. This pattern of self-talk is as unique as our fingerprints; we observe and evaluate events, actions, and outcomes, and we create stories that help us make sense of them. In psychology, the way we stitch these stories together is referred to as our *explanatory style*. As we observe people behaving in certain ways and events unfolding in either random or predictable patterns, we evaluate them with respect to three different parameters:

- Was this event or behavior a result of what I did or what one or more others did?
- Is the resulting condition permanent or temporary?
- Do things like this happen all the time, or was this a rare occurrence?

The events, in most cases, are perceived as neutral when viewed by those who were not involved. When they impact us, however, we create a story to evaluate and explain what happened. Are the events good or bad? Why did they happen? What are the current and future consequences? This is where our explanatory style comes into play. Consider the following event:

One morning, you arrive at work late because of heavy traffic. You immediately go to the staff meeting that started 10 minutes earlier, quickly apologize for being late, and take your seat. Your boss looks directly at you and sarcastically says, "Thanks for gracing us with your presence this morning!" You apologize again and take out your notepad.

How would you "explain" this situation to yourself?

- I'm usually never late, so this is no big deal. He's got a lot on his plate and has a right to be a bit upset, but this will pass. I'll make it up to him somehow later.
- Oh, my God, what have I done? He has it in for me anyway, and this is just one more time I've screwed up. I can tell he's really angry and will probably hold this against me during next week's performance review.

- What's the big deal? So I'm 10 minutes late for a meeting. He's been late, and no one yelled at him. What a jerk he is for singling me out like that!

This is the same event with three different interpretations. As it relates to developing and maintaining healthy self-esteem, it's important that our stories neither damage us nor free us from blame. Rather, they should cause us to see ourselves as human, prone to occasional shortcomings. We should continue to feel worthy, accountable, and capable, thus giving us hope for a successful future. More importantly, it is the mindset that allows us to continue to do our best work.

8. Focus on What You Can Control, Not What You Can't

As I've learned the hard way, our short-term destiny is not always in our control. In the early stages of the great recession, my business practice faced financial challenges it never encountered before. Although I knew better, it did (albeit temporarily) impact my self-esteem. The clients who raved about my great services still raved. The problem was that they weren't calling me to do work for them. Some clients simply disappeared and weren't quickly being replaced by new prospects. Our 2009 revenue came in at less than half that of the previous year. Even though the rational part of my brain told me that this was an anomaly, the emotional side didn't want to listen. It put up a brave front, but conspiratorially whispered that things might not get better. It invented distorted chains of reasoning that concluded that my dream of a successful business might be over, that I might be a failure. As I'm sure it did for many others, this fear got the best of me for awhile.

Even for someone who knows better, unforeseen and unfamiliar changes in our environments can lead to profoundly unsettling emotional responses. We can't predict what tomorrow will bring, let alone next year. Nor can we reliably predict how we will respond when our environments twist, sometimes cataclysmically, around us. What we can do is make a commitment to do our best in whatever environment we find ourselves. We can also make sure that we build strong friendships with knowledgeable people in advance of our needing their wisdom. As the old adage goes, the best time to replace a roof is always before the storm.

CHAPTER 10 Integrity: The Glue That Holds Respect Together

Whether implied or assumed, there is one "super value" that needs to be embraced in order for respect to take root within all levels of an organization. That super value is integrity. This element is so essential that without it none of our other actions associated with respect would be viewed as authentic.

To understand the nature of integrity, it is best to first look at it through the lens of things, not people. Think of integrity in terms of design, process, and structures. For example, consider a simple steel bolt. By itself, it's both insignificant and harmless. When we use the steel bolt in the construction of a bridge, brake pedal, or jet engine, it takes on a whole new level of importance. We assume that it's been: (1) designed and manufactured properly for the application for which it will be used (the right material, hardness, and dimensions), (2) will hold together whatever pieces it connects, and (3) will perform reliably under any imaginable conditions. We also assume that all the pieces around the bolt will do the same. We rely on every *component* used to manufacture an end product to work as expected. When it doesn't, bad things can happen. The failure of one insignificant bolt can weaken an entire structure. If the bolt is in a critical location, its failure can be catastrophic.

When Integrity Fails

In early 2012, my wife spotted some suspicious activity on a recent American Express business account statement. Apparently, an airline ticket to and from Las Vegas had been purchased for the wife of one of our employees. Since this ticket coincided with a business trip that had been taken by the employee, I called him into the office, brought the matter to his attention, and asked for an explanation. Rather than saying that the charge had been a mistake, the employee stammered and launched into a convoluted story about using frequent flyer miles for his own ticket, partial credits he thought it was okay to use and other seemingly bizarre details. Something just didn't smell right.

The further we dug into the matter, the stranger things got. Rather than staying in typical business class hotels, this employee had stayed at high-end, resort-quality properties and ran up significant meal and beverage charges. It started to look like the employee had turned a business conference trip into an extravagant getaway for him and his wife. This led to more questions and even stranger responses. "What conference was this? Do you have a copy of the agenda? Who did you meet with? What did you get accomplished?"

The answers—or rather the lack of answers—made me sick to my stomach. As it turned out, there was no conference. The employee had lied about the entire trip and essentially took a vacation at the company's expense.

It would be difficult to calculate the total financial impact of this event. In addition to launching a formal investigation, asset recovery, and termination proceedings, I then spent countless hours revising our expense account policy. This was followed up by having every other employee sit through a meeting reviewing the policy and signing statements acknowledging both their awareness of acceptable procedures and the consequences for failing to follow them. Because one employee had been dishonest, I was essentially forced to drag all the others on our team through meetings and related activities that were reactively triggered and oriented toward the dishonest behaviors of that one, soon-to-be former coworker. While most members of the team understood why we had to go through this demoralizing and time-consuming exercise, to say that it had damaged the high-trust culture of our quickly growing company would be an understatement.

Not only was there a short-term hit to our productivity, but there was also longer-term damage. Because the fired employee had been the manager of our marketing and communications functions (with someone else reporting to him), we now had a huge hole in our organizational structure. This meant that others would have to chip in (which they gallantly did) and help pick up the slack with at least the most critical of these duties. This then meant that they would have to either work considerably longer to get their own work done or simply drop or postpone some of the less critical tasks.

In retrospect, there were many lessons learned all the way around. First, we probably needed a more formalized expense reporting system with controls at the outset. As a growing organization, clear policy guidelines are important in order to minimize misunderstandings of expectations. Second, it taught me (after 15 years) that you can't always spot "bad apples," no matter how good a judge of character you think you are. As it turned out, I was simply too trusting. Upon further investigation, we found out that this employee had not only repeatedly lied to others (including some of our clients and business partners), but he had been fired from his previous employer for (drum roll please) expense policy violations.

Integrity Is Not Subjective

What does it mean when integrity is applied to human systems? First, let's make an important distinction. Integrity is different from morality and ethics. Both these elements involve subjectivity and judgment. Integrity doesn't, at least not in the same way. Moral and ethical conduct implies adherence to a subscribed set of behaviors that has been deemed just and proper for the members of a specific group or community. The behaviors can vary from group to group. While mission statements and codes of conduct have an important place in defining cultural norms, what works successfully within one company culture (a law firm, for example) could inhibit optimal performance in another (a hospital system). In contrast, integrity is more about how consistently the stated moral and ethical expectations are applied within a culture.

> The supreme quality for leadership is unquestionable integrity. Without it, no real success is possible, no matter whether it is on a section gang, a football field, in an army, or in an office.
>
> Dwight D. Eisenhower, 34th President of the United States

Acting with integrity has several requirements. First, it means that we unconditionally keep or honor our word in all situations. Is there a difference between keeping and honoring? Yes. Sometimes, it becomes impossible to keep a previously made commitment. For example, we promise to attend a meeting on a certain date and time, but we find that we can't because of a canceled flight or family emergency. In this case, honoring our word would require that we do the next best thing. This might include arranging a videoconference or immediately rescheduling the meeting regardless of the unexpected costs these actions might involve.

A second requirement for acting with integrity is that we communicate only what we know to be completely true. This does not mean there won't be times when we can't, for legal reasons, share certain elements of what we know. It also means that we don't allow people to act on assumed information that we know to be false. An example of this would be for a company to continue to promote and sell a product that it knows is unsafe or doesn't perform as advertised.

A third requirement for integrity is that we be clear about our intentions and the reasons behind what we say or do. Related to the previous requirement, this element can be thought of as the "sunshine" clause and involves the transparency of our intentions. If a salesperson recommends a product or service to a client, it should be because it represents the best alternative that he or she can offer to meet the client's needs. If, instead, the recommendation is oriented more toward helping that salesperson win a contest or meet a quota when a better solution is known, then the integrity of the recommendation is in question.

Finally, and perhaps most importantly, integrity requires that we behave in a manner consistent with what we believe to be "right." This includes meeting stakeholder's expectations. If I am a financial advisor, this means that I act in the best interests of my investor clients. If I am a doctor, I make recommendations and suggestions that I believe to be in my patients' best interests. Doing what we believe to be right, even when others around us don't agree, is one of the most courageous actions we can take in the name of integrity.

Arguably, the right thing in any specific situation can be subject to different interpretations based on the competing standards and expectations of various groups of stakeholders. For example, most fast-food restaurants market and sell products they know are inherently unhealthy because of saturated fats, highly processed carbohydrates and caloric density. One could argue that, from the perspective of consumers, it is wrong to sell any products that are scientifically or medically proven to be harmful. On the other hand, anyone who owns stock in these companies rightfully expects that their leaders are doing everything in their collective power to grow revenue and profits. If there is a gray area in determining what is right and what isn't, this is the place. If we are committed to integrity, we are required to make the decisions that impact the majority of our stakeholders favorably. Otherwise, we need to be clear in our communications if we pursue the best outcomes for one particular group over another.

Why is integrity such a significant component of respectful work cultures? At the personal level, the perception of integrity in our actions reinforces the belief by others that they are valued and important. It supports the notion that their ability to work in a predictable environment that takes their well-being into consideration is the primary value guiding our conduct around them. The direct result of this perception is trust, and some level of trust must exist through our interactions with others if we are to achieve a state of respect.

The higher our position within the organization, the more impactful this trust dividend becomes. That's because it sets the tone for our superiors and subordinates. Culture trickles down in an organization, and leadership behaviors set the tone for everyone else. As powerful as personal integrity is for enabling individual engagement, systemic integrity can become a strategic asset. It helps lead to a platform of trust and predictability that encourages an entire organization to engage.

PART III

The Path Forward

CHAPTER 11

A Blueprint for Respectful Organizations

Over the past decade, I have worked with dozens of organizations to help them map out the strategy, resource requirements, and tools for building and sustaining respectful workplaces. Some were large, Fortune 50 companies; others were small; most were for-profit and some were not. The one thing almost all the organizations recognized early was that focusing on respect wasn't a time-constrained initiative. It was a long-range, cultural aspiration to be pursued and protected with the same consistency and energy as any other strategic asset. One client explained it best the following way:

Our organization has four core values. Each is important, but we tend to focus on one or two more consistently than the others. For example, if you were to ask any of our employees or our customers if we are a safe company, we consistently see that over 99% of those asked the question responded with a yes. Safety has been ingrained as a part of our culture for over 100 years. But if you were to ask them if we are a respectful company, the response would be a bit lower. It wouldn't be low, maybe 80%, but it wouldn't be as high as safety. Does this mean we have a problem with respect in our organization? Not at all. It simply means that we have not focused on respect nearly as much as we have safety. You can think of it as a four-legged stool where one or two of the legs are significantly longer than the others. It doesn't make for a very stable platform. Because of the business benefits that we know exist from its pursuit, our long-term goal is for our employees and customers to think of us as a respectful place to work (and vendor with whom to work) just as much as they do a safe place to work.

In order to create and sustain a more respectful workplace, there are four distinct "gates" that must be passed through to successfully enable the transformation. Not coincidentally, they are the same four gates that are required for the success of any cultural initiative. They are:

1. Consensus for taking action
2. Mapping
3. Invitation
4. Cultivation and reinforcement

Gate One: Consensus for Taking Action

In early 2012, the director of training and development for a well-known manufacturing company called my office. His mood was marked by a combination of both frustration and foreboding. A long-time friend, he confided in me that the crap had finally hit the proverbial fan. He had been concerned for some time that the disrespectful attitudes demonstrated by some of the company's senior leaders were making it tough for them to not only attract, but keep, the best talent. A few of the most tenured ones had become so adversarial with each other that it was causing tensions that were felt much deeper into and between their respective departments. They were openly confrontational in staff meetings, shunned each other in public settings, and took advantage of almost every opportunity they could to criticize the work of others. More damaging, by fostering a "we versus they" mindset within their own staffs, they made it uncomfortable for their middle managers to actually support some of their peers in other parts of the business.

The situation had finally reached a breaking point because two of the company's high-potential middle managers turned in their resignations during the same week. In their exit interviews, they were very specific about why they were leaving. They were frustrated and worn out. They wanted desperately to do good work that would help the company be successful, but the tensions and hard feelings caused by their senior leaders had made this all but impossible. Even though they had not been actively looking, each had been contacted separately by a recruiter and, with the offer of a little bit more money (and the hope that the new culture would be better), they were gone. This is what had prompted the call. "We've got to do something," he said. "I think even our CEO now knows that this has now become a liability."

In a 2011 Georgetown University survey of 800 managers and employees in 17 industries, the following was revealed about workers who've been on the receiving end of incivility:

- 48 percent intentionally decreased their work effort
- 47 percent intentionally decreased the time spent at work
- 38 percent intentionally decreased the quality of their work
- 80 percent lost work time worrying about an unpleasant incident
- 63 percent lost work time avoiding the offender
- 66 percent said that their performance declined
- 78 percent said that their commitment to the organization declined

- 12 percent said that they left their job because of uncivil treatment
- 25 percent admitted to taking their frustration out on customers[1]

Regardless of how it happens, organizations typically do not take radical action to change their cultures unless there is a reason. There has to be extreme pain or danger associated with not changing, or there must be the potential for significantly greater success (and happiness) by proactively changing course. Sometimes, these two can go hand in hand. Such is the case when an organization is perceptive enough to pick up on early warning signs that then send its leaders in search of viable, credible options for moving in a new direction. No matter what the impetus is, what's necessary is to arrive at a solid consensus that the cultural status quo is (or could soon be) a liability to the organization's future growth and success. Is your organization ready to take action? Ask yourself a few questions:

1. On a scale of one to ten, how would you rate the strength and value of your organization's culture?
2. As you think about what will be necessary to be successful five years in the future, is your culture an asset or a liability?
3. How strong and supportive are the relationships between your senior leaders? How about between your midlevel managers? How about between individual contributors? Are your employees showing up to work each day looking forward to giving their very best effort and making a difference? If not, why?
4. Compared with other organizations in your industry, how well does yours do at attracting and retaining the most talented employees available?
5. Is your organization the kind of place at which you'd want your own son or daughter to work?

6. If you personally had the chance to make a no-risk move to another company for similar pay but with a more respectful and energizing culture, would you take it?
7. Does feedback from your customers/clients/patients put you at or near the top of your organization's competitors for customer service and loyalty?

Be aware that commitment to change almost always starts out strong. Most leaders know, intellectually at least, that failure to change and improve is a sure path to mediocrity. The challenge of unforeseen obstacles, changes in the economic environment, or naysayers who defend the status quo and resist change (usually passively) can take their toll. I've seen it; I've tried to coach clients through it; I've even wrestled with it in my own organization. The brutal fact is that the majority of organizational change initiatives lose steam and fail.[2]

The best way to maintain both the commitment to change and momentum once activity starts is to make sure that everyone has both a voice and a stake in the process, particularly at the leadership level. As a case in point, I was recently invited to meet with the senior leadership team of a well-known financial services company. Its challenge was that, while not necessarily in danger, its financial performance lagged considerably behind that of its competition and shareholders wanted to see improvement. Intelligent people were in this group, and they knew that they needed to make some significant structural changes, but their greatest change would need to be a top-to-bottom overhaul of the organization's culture. This was a company with almost 100 years of history behind it, and there was a deeply ingrained belief by some that the "old ways" weren't to be changed. When there was actual change, it usually happened very slowly and then only after overcoming significant resistance. The problem was that a long, drawn-out cultural battle was not an option at this point.

The purpose of my being invited was simple. The team was considering whether or not to hire me and my team to help support the cultural change portion of its initiative. The goal? Help facilitate the transition to a more engaged, adaptable, and respectful organization. The questions the team had for me were logical. They were the same ones that most leaders would ask. What would our approach be and what was the rationale? What was our track record? What would the timeline look like? How much would it cost? Could they call others clients with whom we worked?

The meeting, I thought, went well. Having answered most of the questions to the group's satisfaction, I was prepared to close my portfolio, thank my hosts for inviting me in, and head back to the airport. But before I could stand, another hand went up in the air. "I do have one more question," came a voice. It was from "Phil," the senior vice president of operations. I'd been warned about him ahead of time. He had earned a reputation for being the group's self-appointed skeptic and naysayer, especially to ideas that involved change. Since people like this often do their damage behind the scenes, I was actually relieved that he had chimed in with me present. At least I could address his concerns directly. "Surely," Phil opined, "not all of your clients were successful in changing their cultures. In your experience, when initiatives like this don't work, what's the most common reason why?"

My opinion of the man changed instantly. This was actually a very insightful observation and an intelligent question. My response was simple. "You're right, Phil," I admitted. "While our overall track record is better than most, there have been a few clients that didn't quite make the changes we had hoped they would. The good news is that they all failed for the same reason—and hopefully you can learn from them. Look around the room at yourselves. If this company isn't successful in its efforts to change the culture over the next year, it'll be because the people at this table aren't fully committed to working as a team to make it happen." Their smiles and nods to me and each other signaled that the point hit home and they got it. If they didn't change, nobody else would either. We began formally working with the team as clients the very next week.

Gate Two: Mapping

I once heard a college professor observe, "If you don't know where you're going, any road will take you there." Once you've made a solid commitment to change, you're ready to plot the course. For your company to become a more respectful workplace, it is crucial that you determine your starting point. The only way to gauge how your employees are perceived is to ask them, and the traditional method for doing this is through climate or culture surveys. And while there are literally hundreds of competent and proven vendors who can assist with this process, keep in mind that it does not need to be a complicated, expensive ordeal. Surveys don't need to be long to be effective. They just need to ask the right questions.

Whether you collect the data yourself (assuming you have the proper platform and expertise) or partner with another party, be sure that you're gathering feedback on the prevalence of attitudes and behaviors that are specifically associated with respect. These may include listening, supporting, helping, offering advice or constructive feedback, recognizing, rewarding, challenging, treating people fairly and with dignity, honoring boundaries, showing patience, being available, providing necessary resources, being trustworthy, showing interest in others, being courteous, and displaying a friendly demeanor. Keep in mind that cultural norms can often influence the degree to which respectfulness is associated with certain behaviors. This means that ratings for some behaviors desirable in the United States (i.e., direct eye contact or smiling), may or may not be meaningful when you're measuring perceptions of respectfulness elsewhere.

Don't Ask About What Cannot Be Changed

As a word of caution, one of the cardinal rules we try to encourage our clients to follow is to refrain from asking survey participants for opinions or information that leadership is not prepared to act upon.

This includes actual survey questions, as well as demographic questions. For example, if your organization is not prepared to tangibly change its benefits plan, then don't ask people for their opinions on it. If you're not prepared to reexamine incentive pay structures, don't ask about them. When employees (or customers) take the time to share their opinions with us on a particular subject, there is an implicit expectation that action will be taken based on their feedback. I cannot tell you how many employees (and managers) have expressed frustration during focus group meetings because they are asked the same questions every year, and yet nothing ever changes. The result of this frustration is often disillusionment with the process itself and subsequent declining participation rates in future surveys.

Similar to the survey questions themselves are the demographic reference points we ask our employees to volunteer about themselves. Resist the temptation to break your participants into demographic subgroups for which you cannot take discrete action. Technology permits us to query survey responders on everything from their physical location and work shift to their gender, ethnic background, and age subgroup. We can ask them who their manager is, whether they're hourly or salaried, or how long they've worked for the company. But the question is, just how much of this information can be acted upon? If you found out that you had lower perceived respect scores for Caucasian women who were 35–45 years of age, worked on the second shift, and had been with the company for 5–10 years, would you be able to pursue an intervention strategy that targeted just that group? Maybe so, but probably not.

Asking for too much demographic data may allow your survey provider to give you bigger reports and bill you for more consulting time, but the resulting flood of graphs and charts can do more harm than good. First, too much information can often mask the bigger picture and, ironically, lead to inaction. I've seen this over and over again. I can recall one particular healthcare client spending countless hours (which turned into months) reviewing engagement survey data, trying to understand all the ins and outs of what it meant, and then what it should do. By the time the review team was ready to recommend specific action plans, it realized that it would need to start preparing for the next survey round in three months and so decided to recommend doing nothing until then.

Variance Is the Norm

If it has not been specifically measured before, don't be surprised to find that perceptions of respect may vary widely across an organization. With one recent client survey for a 3,000-person insurance company, ratings across 12 functional departments ranged from a high of 4.7 (on a 5 point scale) to a low of 2.3. While reviewing the results, the CEO candidly shared that, albeit imprecisely, he could have predicted which groups would be higher than others. As it turned out, those departments with the highest composite respect scores were the same ones with the lowest levels of employee turnover and the highest performance to plan ratios. This is a simple reminder of how leaders set the tone for their groups' subcultures and how it can directly impact group performance.

Global companies measuring respect (or a broader measure, such as engagement) face an even more complex task of making sense and later acting on the results. In addition to seeing changes across departments and business units, there will also likely be significant differences that reflect the cultural realities that exist in different countries and regions. Whether in parts of the Middle East, Latin America, Asia, or any of the world's other major business regions, the uncomfortable reality is that not every predominant culture is oriented toward or aspires to the universal extension of respect to the different groups that make up its population. As is discussed later, this can require a highly nuanced approach to nurturing corporate values and behaviors that are not necessarily prevalent in their host country cultures.

Data Are Not Knowledge

While we can surround ourselves with a sea of survey data, the real goal is to convert the most important elements into meaningful intelligence and insight that can then be acted upon to foster change. So with data in hand, it is important that the responses be analyzed in a way that illuminates current perceptions, but also explains them. For example, a typical respect survey question might read: "My manager treats all of his or her subordinates equally."

While the responses to this question can be illuminating, they might not provide enough information to be acted upon. A robust data analysis protocol will include regression analysis (see Figure 11.1) on the responses also. This allows for the establishment of relationships between the different response categories. For example, the responses to the above question might correlate positively to the answers for another question: "My manager takes the time to get to know me as an individual."

This would suggest that how a supervisor treats subordinates is influenced by perceptions of how much time he or she spends getting to know each employee. While generating this level of analytical detail admittedly requires more time and effort, it is crucial in helping to point the way to the intervention strategies that will have the best chance of raising respect scores in the future.

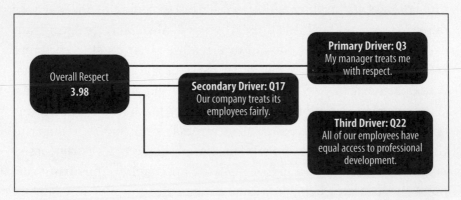

Figure 11.1 Survey driver analysis

Treat Cultural Survey Feedback as Dialogue

Just as important as collecting and analyzing survey data is subsequently acknowledging the time and effort spent by those who generated it. In the broadest sense, a survey represents an invitation to dialogue. The organization asks for opinions and perceptions, and employees answer. But that should not be the end of the conversation. If you or I shared our opinion with somebody about a topic on which we had a significant emotional stake (which, for most of us, includes our work experience), we would expect some kind of follow-up response in real time. In fact, if we gave our opinion to someone and then that someone turned around and walked away, we would understandably be annoyed or possibly even offended. Yet that's exactly what many organizations do every year when they administer employee surveys and then don't offer feedback on the results, sometimes for months. If you want to truly get and keep employees interested in sharing their opinions, start by quickly acknowledging their efforts, telling them what you've learned, and then sharing what you intend to do with the information collected.

My recommended best practice for all clients, no matter how large, is that they report back to their employees in no more than two weeks after a survey is conducted. This initial feedback should include both a summary of the overall results and a short list of the action steps that will be taken in the near future. At the risk of putting some of my survey industry colleagues on the spot, it does not take more than a few days to pull together preliminary survey data once the collection period is over. Because we promise our clients that they will have preliminary data within five business days (it's usually one to two), we ask that they similarly demonstrate a sense of urgency in sharing the information with their employees. When adopted as a standard process metric, this practice increases the perception of transparency in the process itself. Just as importantly, it builds enthusiasm, anticipation, and a readiness for change. Over time, climate surveys should become as natural as breathing. Our experience has been that employees actually look forward to sharing their input and are curious to see the results when they have confidence that they will be used to help improve the quality of their work experience.

Different Tools for Different Tasks

As mentioned earlier, another type of survey tool that can be very helpful is the 360-degree feedback survey for senior leaders, managers, and supervisors. When accompanied by qualified coaching, well-designed 360s are unparalleled in their ability to generate accurate, actionable feedback for individuals responsible for leading others. This is especially important if respect or engagement survey results indicate the need for improvement within certain business units or departments. In these situations, 360s can add invaluable nuance to let leaders know which of their behaviors are either helping or getting in the way of enabling their associates to do their best work. Clarity of perception is priceless. To effectively try to lead a group or organization through a cultural transition without knowing how you are perceived would be like driving a race car at night while wearing sunglasses. You'd better have good insurance.

Gate Three: The Invitation

Similar to a slowly developing friendship, the evolution within an organization toward a climate of greater respect cannot be coerced. Nor would we want it to be. The richest, most enduring cultural attributes in a workplace unfold and then persist because they both support business goals and strengthen the broader stakeholder proposition.

Carrots and Sticks

There are many ways to get people to do what you want them to do. First, you can simply ask or direct them, and possibly offer some explanation for the request. Depending on the nature of what you're trying to get them to do, a second option would be to incentivize them. A third approach, when the request may be contested, might be to use the proverbial "stick." This typically includes the threat of undesirable consequences if they don't comply. A fourth option would be to make the request, and simultaneously provide information or perspective that helps them appreciate the value of what you are asking. Ideally, this would include a clear description of the benefits that would be realized by both them and others.

Consider how you personally might respond or react to the following requests:

1. John, our department didn't do so hot on our last survey round. I need you to start treating your coworkers with more respect.
2. Okay folks, put your smiles on. Whoever in our department ends up with the highest customer satisfaction scores this month will win an extra day of vacation this quarter.
3. Janice, you've already been warned twice. If I hear any more complaints from your peers about foul language, I'll have no alternative but to let you go.
4. Bill, you are one of my very best case managers. If you'd be willing to take a closer look at how your interaction style impacts the cohesiveness and productivity of the rest of your group, I think we'd have one of the very best departments in the company. On top of that, I think we'll all, including you, enjoy working here even more than we already do. Would you be willing to work with me on this?

There are several significant differences between these messages (see Table 11.1): tone, source of motivation, beneficiaries of the request, and time horizon for action.

These differences ultimately have a significant impact on how likely it is that the requests will be followed, as well as whether or not they will result in longer-term behavior change. The first

Table 11.1   Considerations for Influencing Others

	Overall tone	Motivation	Who benefits?	Time horizon
Request 1	Negative	External	Others (maybe)	Until next survey
Request 2	Positive	External (reward)	Me (and hopefully (customers)	This month
Request 3	Negative	External (threat)	Me (keep my job) and others	Immediate
Request 4	Positive	Internal	Me and others	Permanent

three requests, for example, all rely on external (or extrinsic) motivation; the stimulus for taking action is coming from outside of the person (or people) who we want to see changed behaviors. Research has consistently shown that extrinsic motivation, whether based on rewards or punishment, is almost always temporary in its impact. As soon as incentives or fear of punishment go away (or are adjusted to), they lose impact. Rewards have to be increased, and threats eventually cause people to either call our bluff or leave the organization. In addition to being negative in its orientation (our survey scores are low), Request 1 carries no perceived benefit for the recipient and is stated in a way that implies only short-term urgency. Request 2, while positive and likely to result in benefits to both the recipients (financial) and customers (better service), is presented in a way that suggests that we need to bribe our employees in order for them to give their best level of customer service. Request 3 is doomed from the start. While likely the result of ineffective, previous requests, its negative tone and severe consequences may result in short-term compliance, but only as long as other job options are not available.

Out of all the requests, Request 4 has the highest likelihood of being complied with. More importantly, it will likely result in long-term behavior change that does not require continued external pushing by others. The leverage from this type of approach is significant. First, it relies on positive, intrinsic motivation instead of a short-term, extrinsic reward. Provided that the requested action or behavior aligns with his personal values and aspirations (such as being the best manager possible), "Bill" will likely pursue it for its own sake. This is further supported by narrative suggesting that there will be a long-term benefit to both him and others (his group or team). Above all else, the nuance of Request 4 implies a high degree personal autonomy. It does not involve coercion or threats, so Bill has control over whether or not to comply and to what degree. Rather than being bribed, threatened, tricked, made to feel guilty, or otherwise steered into compliance, Bill was *invited* to participate in a developmental journey. This notion of inviting employees to participate in a culture change is foreign to many senior leaders, especially those with strong "command and control" styles. It may even run counter to their personalities, leadership paradigms, and past experiences of being led (or dragged) through change. But make no mistake, the, "You're either on the bus or off the bus" approach has lead to more failed change efforts than successful ones. Why? Because you can't force people (or even a single person) to change if they don't want to. Sure, you can force changes in certain elements of the employee environment. You can blow up reporting structures, change titles, streamline processes, integrate new technology, and move physical locations. As a last resort, you can even get rid of those unwilling to get with the new program. Never mistake compliance for commitment. This approach may lead to compliance (at least over the short term), but it rarely leads to buy-in, support, and active participation. In contrast, a sincere, well-thought-out invitation to participate in a transition to a better place does.

Don't Forget the Directions

Following the collection and analysis of metrics, a clearer picture of your current culture emerges. There will undoubtedly be areas of preexisting strength; some maybe surprising. There will also be areas needing improvement, some at the macro level and some with discrete populations. Whatever the picture, with its unique historical backdrop and statistically illuminated associations and drivers, this is your starting point and an important element to be included with the invitation. "This is where we are, and this is how we got here."

The next element is an aspirational vision of where the organization needs to go and why. Combined with the previous element, your message may sound something like this:

> *Culture has always been important to our company, and how we engage each other is a part of that culture. While not without flaws, it has served us relatively well up to this point. At the same time, what was good enough yesterday doesn't guarantee our success tomorrow.*
>
> *So we invite you to help us move deliberately and enthusiastically in a new direction, one that puts more emphasis on respect as one of our core business values; respect for each other, respect for our clients, and especially respect for ourselves. Why respect? Because out of all our values, consistent and intentional respect helps create a stable platform from which each of us can do our very best work.*
>
> *You've already shared your thoughts with us in our recent survey. You've told us what we're already good at and where we need to improve. Thank you. And now we ask for your active participation to continue the journey, a journey that will benefit you, me, your colleagues, and, in fact, all the stakeholders in our business.*

These may not be the words you choose, but they're a start—reference points to which you can add your team's own creativity. But whatever words your invitation eventually includes, let them truly take an aspirational tone. As human beings, we love to take part in something bigger than ourselves and something that makes us better together. The pursuit of respect does this. In fact, it's one of the keys to getting employees to emotionally invest themselves in their company and to spend their discretionary effort to help it succeed. Similarly, the commitment to pursue respect for all employees is, by default, a commitment to build a workplace environment in which employees are truly seen as invaluable assets to their organization. Show me an employee or manager who doesn't want to be a treated like that, and I'll show you somebody that you can eventually do without.

> You are not here merely to make a living. You are here in order to enable the world to live more amply, with greater vision, with a finer spirit of hope and achievement. You are here to enrich the world, and you impoverish yourself if you forget the errand.
>
> Woodrow Wilson, 38th President of the United States

A lack of leadership commitment and effort almost always spells trouble. Without explicitly stated leadership resolve, a culture shift toward respect (or any other desired quality) will be perceived as just another "program of the month." If this happens, the journey may take much longer—or not be fruitful at all. Because of this, effort put into this phase should serve as a commitment checkpoint. If every member of the senior leadership team can't be counted on to participate, walk the talk, and be open to feedback, it's likely an indication that the organization isn't ready to embrace an initiative of this nature.

The final element of the invitation is the tactical road map that lays out turn-by-turn directions for the journey ahead. Like a trip plan, a well-designed road map creates a timeline for activities (i.e., focus groups, training, progress tracking, etc.), highlights resources, and sets clear behavioral expectations for all those involved. Details such as these minimize confusion, build confidence, and keep the element of control in the hands of those who will make it happen.

A well-designed "respect road map" should answer the following questions for employees:

- What will we be doing?
- How will this make us better?
- When is this going to happen?
- Who will be involved?
- What resources will be allocated for this effort?
- How will this affect me?
- What will be expected from me?

Designed and communicated effectively, the invitation creates a powerful blueprint for change; either focusing on or strengthening the organization's commitment to a consistently respectful workplace. Just as importantly, it challenges employees to become collaborating partners in the process. No true culture change is possible without both buy-in and participation of the individuals who live and work within it. Because a more respectful workplace takes shape one employee at a time, leaders, managers, and individual contributors alike come together to create a workplace culture in which all will take pride.

A Personal Touch

Every so often, my partners and I work with what we call "perfect clients." They come to us for ideas, methodologies, and tools and then they actually use them as intended. Two of our favorite clients put their very best efforts into the invitation process, and it showed. Their CEOs went the extra mile to produce videos featuring themselves personally delivering the "invites." These videos were then shared with participants at the beginning of the training that had been custom designed for them and their colleagues. While the clients will remain anonymous, their employees will no doubt smile as they read these familiar words:

Hi, I'm "Susan Jones," and I want to share some information with you about a very exciting journey we'll be starting shortly. At "Our Company, Inc.," we have always taken great pride in being one of the best companies to work for in the world. I believe that a great work experience for our employees translates into great service for our customers.

Part of creating a consistently great work experience is maintaining a work environment where all of our employees feel respected—respected for their knowledge, their talents, their unique histories and perspectives, and for bringing those incredibly valuable assets to work with them each day.

Over the past few months, we've partnered with Legacy Cultures to design and help roll out an initiative called "It Starts with Respect." The purpose of "It Starts with Respect" is simple. It's to stimulate thinking and increase conversation on the importance of respect for people as a core Our Company, Inc., cultural competency. Along the way, we'll develop a "tool kit" and discover how each one of us can engage ourselves in the active process of creating more respectful workplaces and communities. Just as importantly, we'll work together to determine how we're going to get there.

We'll kick off "It Starts with Respect" shortly with an all-employee survey. The feedback from this process, along with subsequent focus group sessions, will help us better understand current perceptions within our company. Then, based in part on this feedback, we'll kick off classroom training for all our managers and leaders later this fall. For most of you, the contents of the training will be very new and will be presented in a way that makes it relevant personally and professionally.

I'd like to make one important distinction about this effort. "It Starts with Respect" is purposefully not a traditional "diversity" initiative. Because Our Company, Inc., already is a diverse organization, this process will focus on things we share and have in common with one another. It will also provide a jumping off point to help us take the next steps in capitalizing on the incredibly rich perspectives and varied experiences that all individuals bring to the workplace with them every day.

I want to personally thank you in advance for your participation over the upcoming year. I'm sincerely enthused about the process we've developed and look forward to hearing your feedback along the way.

Delivered by their respective CEOs, personalized versions of this message squarely hit the mark with employees. Not only did it result in exceptionally high participation and buy-in, but it created a sense of energy, anticipation, and pride in their organizations.

Gate Four: Cultivation and Reinforcement

Organizational cultures are much like other biological systems. Their overall health and strength can be influenced by both internal factors as well as those in the external environment. When nutrients and other resources required to keep the systems healthy are readily available, the systems flourishes and all of their stakeholders thrive. When critical resources are lacking (or withdrawn), the opposite happens. Individual stakeholders get weak (some may even leave) and the bonds that connect their mutual interests weaken. Arguably the most important duty of any senior leadership team is to act as long-term stewards, safeguarding and strengthening their cultures.

Processes, Tools, and Perseverance

Assuming that there are no casualties up to this point (see Figure 11.2), Gate Four is where the "heavy lifting" begins. In order for rich, pervasive, and enduring respect to take root, the field must be cultivated, and the seeds planted and nurtured.

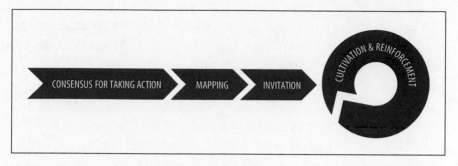

Figure 11.2   Flow arrow diagram

Cultivation takes place on different levels and eventually needs to touch everyone in the organization. The logical starting place is leadership and management. Based on feedback from whatever survey tools were deployed, leaders and key managers need to create action plans to address the identified gaps. The tools used in these plans may include focus groups, communication campaigns, and outside consultants. This also typically includes robust training for leaders, managers, and individual contributors alike.

Poor cultivation will lead to a poor harvest. So making sure that those who accept the invitation have a fertile field to germinate and grow in requires a well-thought-out methodology, the right tools, and patience. It also requires vigilance for obstacles and a feedback loop to chart progress. The tools used are both tactical and administrative. Standard tactical tools include survey instruments (both organizational and 360), focus groups, and well-designed training content, including reinforcement elements and qualified, credible facilitators. Administrative tools and capabilities may include learning management systems (LMS), process mapping and idea-sharing networks, and dedicated coordinators.

The price of inaction is far greater than the cost of making a mistake.

Meister Eckhart, German Theologian, Philosopher, and Mystic

Part of the art of facilitating culture change is managing the direction and part is managing the momentum. As I reflect on the more successful initiatives that I have been a part of, I have to say that momentum is probably a bit more important. The direction is important too, but it can be massaged and adjusted on the fly. Once momentum starts to fade, it's difficult to revive, and the familiar stench of another "flavor of the month" begins to permeate the air. Don't let this happen! Nothing kills momentum faster than a failure to account for shifting priorities or a lack of required resources. Both of these issues need to be discussed, debated, and agreed upon at the front end to make sure they don't bite you in the back end.

One way to buffer against shifting priorities is to designate respect initiative champions who have responsibility for making sure that tasks are completed and milestones met. While not necessarily dedicated 100 percent to the initiative, they do need to be given sufficient time to act as both champions and shepherds. Just as importantly, they should ideally report in this capacity directly to a senior executive (typically in human resources) with ultimate rollout responsibilities. Similarly, make sure these individuals have the resources they need to be successful. Budgets for surveys, training materials, facilitation, intellectual property licenses, and travel need to be determined after establishing outcome measures, not the other way around.

When budgets are tight, organizations are better off rolling out training in smaller chunks to everyone rather than limiting the population to whom training is made available. This slow and steady approach greatly reduces the chance of momentum stalling. It does, however, sometimes result in an unintended consequence: the desire for more. In several instances where large organizational training rollouts were planned to take place over multiyear horizons, early adopters were frequently requesting the next phase of training before some of their peers had started the first phase. While the buy-in and enthusiasm are visible testaments to how hungry employees can be for this kind of training, they're also a reminder. Planning should include having appropriate follow-up and reinforcement elements available soon after the initial training begins. This will eliminate a lot of headaches and scrambling later.

The Secret Sauce: What Makes a Solid Training Curriculum?

1. Viable options will never be a problem. There are literally hundreds of competent training organizations with probably thousands of course offerings to complement your pursuit of more respectful workplaces. Many courses can be delivered either live (including via train-the-trainer), and there are even a handful of decent online offerings that are now coming to market. Suffice it to say, depending upon your needs, timeline, and budget, there are multiple roads to take that could lead to the desired results. So rather than trying to lay out the ideal content model (which would likely mirror the one that my company promotes), let me instead offer some general suggestions. Start with great content for your leaders, including your informal opinion leaders. These people will be the ones whose opinions are first shared with others in your organization. If you nail the content with this group, you can pull the most impactful elements to be used for the broader population. This is also the best group to use outside facilitators. Leaders love hearing from instructors and thought leaders who have worked across multiple organizations and cultures.

2. Focus on the "what" and the "why," but also the "how." Make sure your selected content covers at least basic behavior change methodology so participants have the confidence to step into new, more appropriate behaviors.

3. Consider a blended learning delivery model. Online learning by itself is not suited for building consensus on appropriate respectful behaviors between people who work together. At the same time, exclusive reliance on classroom training can be both time consuming and expensive. Start in the classroom and reinforce online.

4. Consider using a train-the-trainer approach. In addition to being more cost effective than sole reliance on contract trainers, train-the-trainer delivery models allow you to build an infinitely stronger support structure into the overall design of your respect initiative. Those who deliver your training internally tend to be the most enthusiastic supporters and role models.

5. Choose a curriculum partner that has multiple language offerings. Whether you need them immediately or not, there's a good chance that you will in the future. Our global clients routinely require that content intended for use by individual contributors be available in 25-plus languages.

6. Include content that is not singularly applicable to the work environment. If you really want your people to get excited about respect, show them how to migrate the same concepts into their personal lives. Regardless of where they use them first, a skill practiced is a skill mastered (except for golf).

7. Make it novel, keep it fun, and allow it to be collaborative. If respect training simply becomes code for repackaged diversity training that you already rolled out (but with a new cover), you'll lose people fast. With all the new data to inform this topic from neuroscience, anthropology, and psychology, there's more than enough content to make your curriculum relevant, upbeat, and fresh. Similarly, keep a "we" orientation around key takeaways and action plans. Culture is defined by the unique set of behaviors and interaction patterns that define an organization or team. Let your participants lend their voices to in order to influence what tomorrow's respect-based culture should look like.

I offer one specific content suggestion for increasing collaboration and building consensus for respect within intact teams. Referred to as a Code of Cooperation, this facilitated group exercise is designed to give employees who work together an equal voice in determining the behavioral norms that define their ideas of a respectful workplace. While there may be general guidelines that all employees must follow, like the organization's existing code of conduct or ethics policies, each group's Code of Cooperation document instead reflects the unique personality of its creators. It includes both behaviors they expect of each other and behaviors they expect each other to refrain from.

The trade-off with this method of codifying behavioral norms is one of consistency versus adherence. While it's assumed that there may be variations between Codes of Cooperation created by different groups within an organization, the likelihood that these documents will be supported goes up exponentially because of their unique content. People support what they help create. It is very empowering and esteeming to give a group the ability to voice its own ideas of what respect should look like for its members.

A Plan for the Ages

Culture change in pursuit of greater respect is tricky. Its benefits may be hard to imagine up front, it can take significant resources to facilitate, and it doesn't happen overnight. For managers and leaders, it takes discipline, personal accountability, and courage. It takes discipline to gain consensus, allocate resources, and methodically go through all four gates of the plan. It takes a personal commitment to present model behaviors that are consistent with the preferred culture. Mostly, it takes courage; courage to acknowledge our own needs for improvement, courage to make ourselves vulnerable to others as we embrace and practice new behaviors, and courage to say we're sorry when we miss the mark.

But the payoff for our efforts, both organizationally and personally, is handsome indeed. Organizations that embrace respect for people as one of their guiding values outperform their competitors in almost every area. They attract and retain better talent, they innovate faster, they serve and satisfy their clients more effectively, and they adapt to changing economic and competitive climates more quickly. Leaders who embrace respect as a core value facilitate these advantages. They are more trusted, more influential, and more effective at fully leveraging their organizations' human assets. As a personal bonus, they also tend to be happier, physically healthier, and more upwardly mobile in their careers. The pursuit of respect is a perfect culture plan for the ages.

Pursuing Respect Globally

The more diverse a population, the greater the effort and coordination required for cultivating respect as a cultural strength. Consider the immense challenges faced by Johnson Controls, Inc. (www.JCI.com). Based in Milwaukee, Wisconsin, the company is a global provider of products and services that include everything from automotive batteries and HVAC (Heating, Ventilation and Air Conditioning) systems, to military hardware for the U.S. government and contract building services. It employs over 168,000 workers in 150 countries and has facilities on every continent, including Antarctica. Perceptions of what respect should look like can be significantly different in Singapore from the way they are in Toledo, Ohio, or Riyadh, Saudi Arabia. Still, creating a culture of respect is an effort that the company willingly makes because of its importance to business success.

According to Fernando Serpa, director of global diversity and inclusion for Johnson Controls, during a personal interview: "It's all about business results. In order for us to meet our production and performance goals, it's crucial that our managers and employees respect and appreciate the differences between themselves and their peers."

So important is treating others with respect that it's included as one of the company's 10 "must have" competencies in the Johnson Controls Leader Expectations Model. This means that every employee in a leadership position, be he or she a front-line supervisor or country business unit president, is rated and coached on how to become more proficient at treating subordinates, peers, and even clients with respect. Behavior ratings on this competency can range from a minimum of "acceptable" (includes: being open to new ideas) to "strength" (includes: willing and able to change in response to different viewpoints), up to "exceptional" (includes: builds effective relationships with people, including those with different experiences and backgrounds).

Just because a certain behavior set is stated and measured, however, doesn't mean that it always comes without growing pains. "There are sometimes unwritten behavioral rules for a given culture that run counter to our goal of a consistent commitment to respect across the different business enterprises," said Fernando. "They may vary from country to country, or even within the same country. Our facilities in the Middle East, for example, have somewhat different behavioral norms than our corporate offices in Milwaukee." He then went on to share a specific example from a previous employer of how shifting demographics had led to cultural differences at one plant that resulted in perceptions of disrespect between different groups. The result was a significant drop in productivity. "But when we actually got the different groups to sit down together and collaboratively define what respect should look like going forward, we saw an almost immediate improvement in performance. This same approach can be used in any almost any organization."

Looking to the future, what lessons have been learned at Johnson Controls that might help other companies build respect as a core cultural competency? "Two things are crucial," offered Fernando. "To build the required support, you have to have to tie respect directly to the successful pursuit of business goals. Secondly, you have to focus on, measure, and reinforce specific behaviors. Respect means many different things

continued

to different people depending on their backgrounds, so you have to be precise with the exact behaviors you want to see." Challenges notwithstanding, the effort is worth it because respect allows the company to bring out the best in all of its employees. And that is a nonnegotiable for continued success in a globally competitive marketplace.

Respect as a Customer Service Strategy

Respect for employees can easily be leveraged into something else that impacts business—respect for customers. In late 2012, my wife and I decided to take our family on an impromptu vacation. Her father had passed away just a few months earlier, and the ensuing tsunami of raw emotions, funeral preparations, visiting family, and estate settlement tasks (not to mention our already-planned work obligations) left us literally drained and with little energy left to give our kids. We wanted to go someplace with just the four of us that would allow us to give them our undivided attention. Since we all had passports, someplace in Mexico sounded like a good idea, and we could get direct flights into several major cities.

Both of us had stayed at Ritz-Carlton hotels for business before, but neither of us had done so for pleasure, so we decided to give the Cancun property a try. Although the trip would be for only four days, we had both had good experiences with Ritz-Carlton in other cities and wanted as much of a "no hassles" trip as possible. As it turned out, our expectations were not only met, but wildly exceeded. In fact, this one hotel experience recalibrated my perceptions of what levels of customer service are actually possible and how respect can play a key role in its pursuit.

The pleasant surprises began the minute we arrived at the hotel. Upon exiting the shuttle from the airport, my wife and I were both greeted by name by the bellman, who told us that all arrangements for our bags were already taken care of. After checking in, we then were escorted to the club level floor where we could refresh and change clothes while our room was being readied. Imagine the pleasant look of surprise on my children's faces when they were similarly greeted by the floor concierge and offered fruit smoothies to begin their stay. My wife and I had similar expressions when we were handed cold wash towels to clean our hands followed by just-poured glasses of champagne. We were at the hotel barely 15 minutes, and we already felt like the vacation was well underway.

Over the next few days, the VIP treatment just got better and better. By the end of the second day, it seemed that all members of the staff knew each of us by name. They also were making mental notes about our preferences because they seemed to anticipate what we wanted before we even asked. "Ryan, would you like water again with your lunch? And Mr. Meshanko, a cold Negra Modelo?" I hate to admit it, but we were being completely spoiled and loved every second of it! In retrospect, what made the experience so extraordinary was the endless combination of little things that the staff members did and how they did it. It was almost as if they delighted in surprising us with new, small ways of making our stay enjoyable each day; milk and treats left on the table for the kids with the turn-down service, fresh towels offered when we headed to the beach from the pool, my iPhone returned to our room when I left it at the dinner table, or a fresh, hot cup of decaf coffee with a just-baked cookie offered to my wife when she was sitting in the lobby reading a book one evening.

Just as important as these acts of service were the accompanying gracious attitudes. Every single employee had mastered the arts of smiling, laughing, and making solid, unwavering eye contact. From the concierge (who had been on staff with this property for almost 14 years) to the pool and cleaning staffs, they were singularly focused on each guest with whom they spoke. This simple demonstration of attention by itself seems like a rarity these days.

As with most vacations, the days went by quickly. When we returned from breakfast on our last day, our bill had been slipped under our door, just the way it is with most hotels. But with our bill, there was something else included—a typed up thank-you card from the hotel with handwritten, personal comments from each of the staff members who had served us during the past few days. The impression they had created was that we were more than just hotel guests. We were the Meshanko family and, with all of our personalities and preferences, were uniquely memorable. As if scripted to match our earlier suggested definition of respect, the Ritz-Carlton staff had collectively engaged each of us in a way that made us feel welcomed, valued, and special.

A logical question to ask at this point is, how does any company cultivate such an amazing customer service experience? It certainly doesn't happen by accident. In the case of the Ritz-Carlton, it's actually built into the very fabric of the company's culture. Consider the company's credo (akin to a mission statement), which is just one element of its renowned Gold Standards:

The Credo

The Ritz-Carlton Hotel is a place where the genuine care and comfort of our guests is our highest mission.

We pledge to provide the finest personal service and facilities for our guests who will always enjoy a warm, relaxed, yet refined ambience.

The Ritz-Carlton experience enlivens the senses, instills well-being, and fulfills even the unexpressed wishes and needs of our guests.

Accompanied by the matching motto, three steps of service, and (12) service values, this framework creates a virtual road map for creating the same experience my family had for practically every guest.

Even with a compelling mission statement and set of values, words can be cheap. Most of us work (or have worked) for other organizations with similarly lofty mission statements and slogans about exceptional customer or patient service. In too many cases, that is all that they are—statements that sounded good to whoever thought them up but that failed to translate into the behaviors and actions necessary to generate results. The personal commitment by each employee to consistently perform and serve in accordance with this road map is possible only when then the employees are treated by their leaders and managers with similarly high standards.

Ritz-Carlton knows that it must practice what it preaches. As my family was being driven to the airport that final morning, I struck up a conversation with our driver. Not a Ritz-Carlton employee himself, he worked for a company that was contracted by the local hotels to safely transport their guests to and from the airport. To pass the time, I asked him how he liked his job. He said, "It's okay. The work isn't too hard, and I meet nice people." Then he continued with a grin, "But I'd really like to get a job at the Ritz. They treat their people better than any other company in Cancun." I'm quite sure that they do.

Create Your Own Ritz-Carlton Experience

It should come as no surprise that some of the companies with the highest ratings in customer service are also some of the financially most successful in the world. Winners of the 2012 Customer Service Hall of Fame Awards[3] include companies such as Amazon, Google, Apple, Sony, Hilton Hotels, American Express, FedEx, Marriott Hotels, and Southwest Airlines. In fact, if your 401k portfolio contained only stocks of the companies that excelled at delivering A+ customer service, you'd be wealthy! According to research conducted by Professor Claes Fornell from the University of Michigan's School of Business Administration, companies with the highest ACSI (American Customer Satisfaction Index) consistently outperformed other publicly traded companies. Dow Jones (DJIA) companies outperformed their peers by 93 percent, S&P 500 companies by 201 percent, and NASDAQ companies by 335 percent.[4]

If your organization were to create its own version of a Ritz-Carlton experience for its customers, what would it look like? Who would be involved? What behaviors would be emphasized? How might it change your actual business processes? How would you measure your progress? Which of your business metrics would most likely improve? How would this affect how your company interacts with its vendors and suppliers? Most importantly, what kind of internal behavior standards would need to set be in place first? Without respect on the inside, consistent respect on the outside simply isn't sustainable.

Don't Expect Perfection

Just as the proverbial road to hell is paved with good intentions, the road to respect occasionally finds itself in need of repair. Potholes, obstacles, and detours can be expected. Competitive threats, financial obstacles, technology shifts, and the occasional leaders who don't grasp the "people thing" will sometimes put culture in the backseat.

The good news is that the cultural norms that resonate best for most people tend to be enduring. Whether they are respect, integrity, safety, or customer focus, some values and their associated behaviors simply lead to stronger, smarter, and more adaptable businesses.

When it Doesn't Work, Throw it Out

Dealing with deeply-entrenched cultural challenges often requires more than a good strategy and the right tools. Sometimes, you need a broom first. Such was the case with an international electronics manufacturer. When the new manager of sales training was hired, he was consoled by some of his peers. It seemed that his group had a reputation for being hard to work with. Associates wished him luck, and he soon found out he was going to need it.

The first few months on the job were rough. Staff meetings were dysfunctional, people routinely showed up late, and hostility between key members of the team was normal. Efforts to exert some sort of control and positive influence over the group were only marginally successful, and the group's overall productivity was poor. At one point, the manager found himself being pulled into the drama he inherited and "lost it" during a meeting. Something had to change.

That watershed moment proved to be the catalyst for change that was needed to propel the manager onto a different path. It became clear that some of the relationships between his key reports were too badly damaged to be repaired. The disrespect demonstrated between them wasn't just "surface rust." The years of neglect and the corrosive attitudes and behaviors had resulted in structural damage that the key players themselves weren't even interested in fixing. The resulting toxicity rubbed off on everyone with the by-products of low group morale, projects that took far too long to complete, and mediocre quality of programming.

The key players knew there was a problem, but they were too stuck to move on their own. The manager met with each one individually to see where their hearts were. During these nonthreatening and reflective meetings, they concluded that they weren't where they needed to be for either their personal or the team's success. Each employee independently decided it was time for a change. No tearful terminations, no expensive severance packages, and more importantly no animosity.

The message to the remaining team members was clear. The old behavioral norms weren't acceptable. The group's work on behalf of the company was too important to be compromised by people who either couldn't or wouldn't work well together. Mutual respect, a positive attitude, and accountability became the new cultural norms, and performance flourished within months.

There Are No Shortcuts to Respect

As with most most worthy pursuits, the journey to creating a respectful work culture takes deliberateness driven by the belief that such a pursuit is in the best long-term interest of the enterprise. It also takes time, attention to detail and perseverance. The four-gate model just described is not a panacea and certainly not presented as a shortcut to success. It's a long-range methodology for aligning and leveraging the discrete disciplines of business strategy, organizational development, psychology and neuroscience. When done properly, the results can be both transformational and transcendent, with culture and values becoming the bedrock of all future business activity.

CHAPTER 12 Respect Outside of Work

A s important as the pursuit of respect is in the global workplace, it is no less important in our homes and communities. The two really can't be separated if there is to be any sustainable change in the workplace. I am sure that I'm not the first to notice that respect and civility seem to be taking a backseat to expediency in our high-tech, high-volume society. You can sense it in our interaction styles, the "in your face" behaviors glamorized on our television shows, and, regrettably, in the increasingly negative tone of our political discourse. The same rules of neuroscience that determine workplace productivity also dictate the output and accomplishments of societies and nations. Energy that is spent criticizing, demeaning, and otherwise tearing down our fellow citizens is energy that can't be spent to build.

Family and Friends

Any book focusing on the use of respect to leverage culture, emotions, and neuroscience to build a better business wouldn't be complete without addressing what happens when employees leave the office. Long work days, busy extracurricular schedules, dual career paths, and smartphones in people's pockets can hinder engaged, respectful home environments. Nostalgia aside, something seems to have been lost from the family experience over the past few decades. On the decrease is the undivided, one-on-one attention that we used to give each other. Some will say that this is an over-broad generalization; that attention gaps of various names have existed in every modern society. To this observer, it appears we are hell-bent on multitasking ourselves right out of the respect, curiosity, and thoughtfulness that have been the hallmarks of civilized society for thousands of years.

I remember as a child in the late 1960s how frustrated my mother would get with my father. No matter how much she pleaded, she found it almost impossible to convince him to participate in a family dinner without the evening news playing on his 12-inch, Sylvania black-and-white television set. Even then, the hypnotic pull of television competed for the attention of those sitting just a few feet away from us, and it frequently won. Today, that competition is all but over. No matter what the venue, the familiar glow of televisions and smartphones can be seen intruding upon and interrupting almost every venue for social interaction. Restaurants, theaters, kitchen tables, living rooms, elevators, passenger seats, and nightstands are all fair game. It has been with some amusement that I've seen people sneaking a peak at their mobile devices in houses of worship and restrooms. I suspect that it's only a matter of time before our most private encounters are routinely interrupted by our favorite songs and ringtones, and we won't think twice about whether or not it's okay to respond.

Far from shunning technology, I say let's embrace it—with boundaries. When we talk with our spouses, partners, kids, or friends, let's do it face to face whenever possible, without our trigger fingers waiting for the first hint of vibration from our pocket. Let's make time to connect with those closest to us. Whether during dinner, family outings, or simple walks around the block, let's commit to validating each other by sharing the two commodities for which there are no surrogates—time and attention. With two preteen children, I'll be the first to admit that I still need some practice when it comes to being fully present in my family interactions. I'm hoping that intention will at least nudge me in the right direction.

There are several reasons why it is important that we display respect and civility with our family and friends. First, those closest to us deserve our absolute best. Second, remember the paths our brains form from repeated behaviors? Being consistently respectful both at work and at home reinforces the positive behaviors we strive to make permanent. The more we practice civility, the greater the chance it becomes second nature in every aspect of our lives. Finally, because of our close relationships, our family and friends are probably more forgiving than our employers and coworkers. That doesn't mean that my wife (or my children) should expect less attention and respect from me than I give my employees.

Our Political Dialogue

Nowhere is the insidious creep of incivility and disrespect more apparent than in our political processes. And, nowhere besides our private-sector workplaces is the need for respect greater. What used to be subtle, ideological, and/or philosophical differences have been replaced by stark, inflexible labels. What used to be known as political discourse and debate has been replaced by "villainization," smear tactics, and outright lying. Add virtually unlimited financial resources to broadcast and disseminate this misinformation, and you have a recipe for the slow, steady meltdown of our current systems of governance. The short-term victims of the tactics of negativity are solid, decent candidates and important legislation that benefits the citizens of our world's democracies. But when personal vendettas publicly trump doing what's best for the long-term good of the nation, the real victims are "we the people." An example of this divisive mindset was on public display when Mitch McConnell, Senate Minority Leader opined that "The single most important thing we want to achieve is for President Obama to be a one-term president."[1]

Having recently emerged from what can best be described as a bruising 2012 presidential election in the United States, it's hard not to be critical of the extraordinarily toxic mix of political advertisements that blanketed the airwaves leading up to election day. Those who lived in one of the so-called "battleground states" (such as Virginia, Ohio, and Wisconsin), were probably inclined to unplug their television sets at some point. Yet the more we complained and told pollsters that we detested these angry, vicious, and often misleading commercials, the more frequently they came. The reason was simple. Research shows that negative political ads work. In fact, they work amazingly well.

Negative ads about both candidates and issues are effective because of how our brains process information.[2] They are designed to evoke the powerful emotions of fear, anger, distrust and disdain, and attach them to an opponent's candidate or issue. Their goal, however, is not to change peoples' minds about their candidates. Their goal is to discourage the supporters of the attack ad targets from voting at all. It's a literal race to the bottom. Since almost all major political actors and agents participate in this mind-numbing duel of diatribe, none of us come out unscathed. The barrage of repetitive, negative messages from multiple angles and aimed at numerous targets is emotionally draining and simply causes many to disconnect from the political process entirely. Ironically, rather than increasing participation in democracy, these tactics and strategies actually weaken democracy because they make it distasteful for voters. Is there a place for criticism and the healthy competition of ideas and ideologies that will determine the future of our countries? Of course there is. In fact, the bedrock of our democratic principles is our ability to present differing visions and priorities for our future. In the increasingly Darwinian environment of super PACs (Political Action Committees), almost limitless campaign contributions and 24/7 news coverage, the goal is for a candidate or position to win. As the political arena becomes progressively more uncivil, hopefully people will notice, grow tired of these tactics, and simply tune out the messages of fear and anger.

Respect Is About Me

> Thousands of candles can be lighted from a single candle, and the life of the candle will not be shortened. Happiness never decreases by being shared.
>
> Hermann Hesse, German-Swiss Poet, Novelist (Siddharta), Painter

All paths we take toward others eventually circle back to us. Even if you personally make the commitment to practice respect, not everyone you meet has done the same. Some won't take the time and energy necessary to engage you or find common ground on issues. Others may not demonstrate that they value you as a person. They'll show up late for important meetings, interrupt you while you speak, and harshly criticize your ideas without being brave enough to offer their own. There will be those who occasionally yell and use vulgar language, attack you personally, and lie. There are also individuals who will say or do things we interpret as disrespectful not out of malice or spite but simply out of ignorance. When we commit to a path of respect, we do so in spite of these eventualities because it reflects who we are at our core.

Respect is about you and me, not "them," and our commitment to it influences everyone around us. Once we understand the value proposition respect offers, that insight can provide us with patience, courage, and creativity. Patience permits us to maintain our composure and respectful demeanor when others are not acting at their best. Courage enables us to candidly challenge disrespectful behaviors and actions directed toward others. Creativity allows us to see points of connection, even in the midst of conflict. When we bring these qualities online and into our work interactions, everyone benefits, including our peers, customers, vendors. and ultimately, our shareholders.

Once again, I think back to my college dorm director, mentor, and friend, Dale, and am thankful that he showed me respect even when I didn't necessarily deserve it. In retrospect, he likely did so as much for himself as he did for me; it was simply an active demonstration to himself of the person he chose to be. I just happened to be a lucky recipient. I'd also like to think that his commitment to himself paid future dividends through me to my current colleagues and others whom he'll never meet.

Final Thoughts

Emotions can be triggered in the blink of an eye and by the subtlest of cues. Their impact on our performance is profound and sometimes lasting. I've been the receiver of respect many times over and benefited from its afterglow. I've also tasted my share of disrespect and was sent into a downward spiral of anger, frustration, fear, or apathy. Simply paying attention to how others' behaviors impact us can help to keep our awareness of our own behaviors in clearer focus. It also reminds us of how inextricably linked to each other we will always be.

Just as there are many reasons compelling us to elevate respect to a higher level of social and professional importance, there are many obstacles to achieving that goal. Time pressures, competing agendas, lack of awareness, our sometimes low sense of self-worth, or physical exhaustion can all cloud our ability to treat each other with the respect and dignity we deserve. Unfortunately, the costs of these shortcomings to business are great. Lawsuits, low productivity, high turnover, poor customer satisfaction, and diminished resilience are just the tip of the iceberg. The bottom-line impact of diminished physical health, compromised trust, and stifled creativity may never be fully appreciated.

With so much at stake, why would any business or society not strive to get better? The simple reason is inertia. Change is difficult, self-interest more convenient, and the status quo far easier to maintain. This in no way means that change is impossible. If it were not, humans would never have made it as far as we have. Nor does it mean that we can let ourselves off the hook from trying. To the contrary, the battle for respect is very winnable and more than pays for itself in increased shareholder value. For many organizations, it already has. As a follow-up to the earlier profile on E.I. DuPont (see Cultivating Respect as a Global Value in Chapter 6), I checked in with the company's Respect for People champions at the end of 2012 to see how their efforts were progressing. Ana Somolinos, Respect for People champion representing the company's Europe, Middle East, and Africa (EMEA) operations, offered the following in a personal correspondence:

> *DuPont embarked on the RSS (Respect—Source of Our Strength) deployment journey in the middle of 2011 as a way to build a robust foundation and raise the bar relative to RFP (Respect for People), one of the 4 Core Values of the Corporation. Key to this effort was conveying the message that Respect starts with each one of us and requires that we pay greater attention to and invest positive energy into our interactions with each other.*
>
> *Over the past 24 months, more than 40,000 DuPont employees globally have participated in and completed this powerful and introspective workshop. The feedback collected has been both hopeful and, in many cases, inspiring. Our employees are learning to look into this space with a renewed, open lens. Importantly, they feel empowered to grow both personally and professionally.*
>
> *As gratifying as it has been to hear the positive personal feedback from our employees, the RSS initiative is very much a business growth strategy enabler. Employees emotionally connect and contribute hard to an organization which values and allows them to grow as both human beings and professionals. We believe that the RSS process positively impacts our Employee Value*

Proposition and strengthens our ability to retain and attract the best talent in the market place. RSS continues to be an unforgettable journey for our Corporation and has become instrumental in impacting the way we conduct businesses internally and externally.

While I've shared a few, there are numerous other examples of other companies that have also made great progress in their pursuit of respect. Most are now the beneficiaries of measurably improved culture scores, more engaged workforces, and healthier bottom lines. Maybe even more importantly, these companies are helping to raise expectations for a new generation; expectations that we all stretch ourselves just a bit more to engage one another in ways that allow all of us to be and do our best. What's holding you back from joining them?

> Never doubt that a small group of thoughtful, committed people can change the world. Indeed, it is the only thing that ever has.
>
> Margaret Mead, American Cultural Anthropologist

Appendix

Sample Affirmative Reminders

The following collection of Affirmative Reminders are intended to assist the reader in properly designing their own. Feel free to use them in their current form or modify them to fit the particulars of your own life situation, values and goals.

Teamwork

I enjoy the feeling I get when I work collaboratively with my team members. Building on each others' ideas, offering constructive feedback, and helping each other be successful makes me feel part of something much bigger than me alone.

I'm good at what I do and even better when I work with others. It makes me feel proud to do my very best work and positively encourage others to do the same because the cumulative effect is nothing short of spectacular.

Recognition and Appreciation

I make time each day to look for and recognize the small contributions that my peers and subordinates make that help our business. I know that they appreciate the recognition, and it makes me feel great inside to give it.

Empathy and Support

More and more, I make the effort to pay attention to the emotional status and needs of my peers. Letting them know that they can count on me to be supportive and lend an occasional hand when things get tough helps all of us.

Listening

Every person in our organization is intelligent and has information, ideas, and perspectives that make us more effective as a team. Because of this, I listen more than I talk and look for opportunities to build on and support the contributions of my coworkers. While we're all smart individually, together we're brilliant.

Patience

I breathe slowly, relax, and remind myself that the road to success rarely follows a straight line. By taking setbacks in stride and accepting small, personal imperfections as part of the game, I keep my eye on our long-term goals and continue to give my best work and highest energy.

Body Language

I remind myself each day to make sure that my face and body are communicating the energy and camaraderie that I feel inside. I stand straight, smile, and present a body posture that tells others that I am present and available to them.

Dignity and Value

Just like me, each of my coworkers represents a unique combination of skills, experiences, perspectives, and know-how. I take great pride in paying attention to the "little things" and looking for opportunities to point out to them how I see them using their unique gifts to make us a better company.

Being Human

Nobody is perfect, including me. When I know that I have made a mistake, I take responsibility, apologize if necessary, and then correct the error. My team counts on me to give my best effort and that's exactly what I strive to give.

More and more, I find it easy to relax, smile and be patient with myself. Like everyone around me, I am a "human becoming." I learn from my mistakes and take setbacks in stride.

The words "I'm sorry" are always close at hand. If I ever treat people poorly, I own my shortcoming, forgive myself, and then apologize quickly and sincerely. Healthy relationships are based on trust, and I do my best to protect them.

Reaching Out

I regularly look for opportunities to introduce myself to and get to know new employees in our company. Sharing a cup of coffee or lunch to get to know people better is easy to arrange, makes our new associates feel welcomed, and helps me expand my personal network of friends and future collaborators.

Notes

Chapter 2

1. Daniel Goleman, *Primal Leadership*. 1st ed. (Boston: Harvard Business Press, March 15, 2002).
2. Jason Marsh, Rodolfo Mendoza-Denton, and Jeremy Adam Smith, *Are We Born Racist? New Insights from Neuroscience and Positive Psychology* (Boston: Beacon Press, 2010).

Chapter 3

1. Adrienne Fox (quote by Ellen Weber), "The Brain at Work, *HR Magazine*, http://www.shrm.org/Publications/hrmagazine/Editorial Content/Pages/3Fox-Your%20Brain%20on%20the%20Job.aspx.March 1, 2008.
2. Gallup, "Employee Engagement: A Leading Indicator of Financial Performance," http://www.gallup.com/consulting/52/employee-engagement.aspx
3. Paul Marciano, *Carrots & Sticks Don't Work*, 1st ed. (New York: McGraw-Hill, June 2010).
4. Roizen, Michael and Oz, Mehmet, *You Being Beautiful: The Owner's Manual to Inner and Outer Beauty* (New York: Free Press , 2008)

Chapter 4

1. "Sucking Up to the Boss May Move You Up and Keep You Healthy," *Science Daily,* June 9, 2011, http://www.sciencedaily.com/releases/2011/06/110609112426.htm.
2. Captain D. Michael Abrashof, *It's Your Ship* (New York: Warner Books, 2002)

Chapter 5

1. Ed Pilkington, "Fox Most Trusted News Channel in US, Poll Shows," January 27, 2010, http://www.guardian.co.uk/world/2010/jan/27/fox-news-most-popular.

2. Alpha-men.net.

3. Paul Zak, *The Moral Molecule: The Source of Love and Prosperity* (New York: The Penguin Group 2012)

4. Annals of Mathematics, Vol. 54, No. 2, Sept, 1951. See: http://www.eecs.harvard.edu/~parkes/cs286r/spring02/papers/nash-cornell.pdf

5. "Five Year Olds Are Generous Only When They're Watched," *Science Daily*. October 31, 2012. http://www.sciencedaily.com/releases/2012/10/121031214138.htm

6. Paul Zak, *The Moral Molecule: The Source of Love and Prosperity* (New York: The Penguin Group 2012)

7. David Livingstone Smith, *Less Than Human: Why We Demean, Enslave, and Exterminate Others*, (St. Martin's Griffin, 2011.

8. Robert A. Burton, *On Being Certain-Believing You Are Right Even When You're Not* (New York: St. Martin's Press, 2008).

Chapter 6

1. Robert K. Greenleaf, *What Is Servant Leadership?* http://www.greenleaf.org/whatissl/.

2. Courtesy Legacy Business Cultures, 2011. http://www.legacycultures.com/2012/01/09/dupont-cultivates-respect-as-a-global-asset

Chapter 7

1. Robert A. Burton, M.D., *On Being Certain, Believing You Are Right Even When You're Not.* (St. Martin's Press, 2008) p. 12.

2. *Forty-seven percent of Americans think gay is a life choice*, December 18, 2009, http://open.salon.com/blog/gaypersonsofcolor/ 2009/12/18/forty-seven_percent_of_americans_think_gay_is_a_life_choice.

3. http://www.goodreads.com/author/quotes/9843.Eric_Hoffer.

4. Jason Marsh, Rodolfo Mendoza-Denton, and Jeremy Adam Smith. *Are We Born Racist? New Insights from Neuroscience and Positive Psychology* (Boston: Beacon Press, 2010).

Chapter 8

1. W. B. Carpenter, *On the Influence of Suggestion in Modifying and Directing Muscular Movement, Independently of Volition,* March 12, 1852, http://www.sgipt.org/medppp/psymot/carp1852.htm.
2. Richard M. Suinn, "Visual Motor Behavior Rehearsal: The Basic Technique," *Scandinavian Journal of Behaviour Therapy* 13 (3), 1984.
3. Victor Pendleton, "Psychologically Speaking: Affirmative Reminders," *The Panther* [student newspaper of Prairie View A&M University] updated June 29, 2011.
4. Adrienne Fox (quote by Ellen Weber), "The Brain at Work," *HR Magazine,* March 1, 2008, http://www.shrm.org/Publications/hrmagazine/EditorialContent/Pages/3Fox-Your%20Brain%20on%20the%20Job.aspx.
5. *Motivating Goal-Directed Behavior Through Introspective Self-Talk: The Role of the Interrogative Form of Simple Future Tense.* Ibrahim Senay, Delores Albarracin & Kenji Noguchi. Copyright 2010. Association of Psychological Science.

Chapter 9

1. "No Difference in Women's and Men's Self-Esteem in Youth and Early Adulthood, Study Finds," *Science Daily,* July 15, 2011, http://www.sciencedaily.com/releases/2011/07/110714120714.htm.

Chapter 11

1. "Rude Behavior at Work Is Increasing and Affects the Bottom Line," *Science Daily,* January 30, 2013, http://www.sciencedaily.com/releases/2013/01/130130184048.htm?utm_source=feedburner&utm_medium=email&utm_campaign=Feed%3A+sciencedaily%2Fliving_well+%28ScienceDaily%3A+Living+Well+News%29.
2. Michael Beere and Nhitin Noria, "Cracking the Code of Change," *(Harvard Business Review,* May 2000)
3. Karen Aho, "2012 Customer Service Hall of Fame," *MSN Money,* http://money.msn.com/investing/2012-customer-service-hall-of-fame-1.
4. Claes Fornell, Sunil Mithas, Forrest V. Morgeson III, and M. S. Krishnan, "Customer Satisfaction and Stock Prices: High Returns,

Low Risk," *Journal of Marketing*,. January 2006,. http://terpconnect.umd.edu/~smithas/papers/mithascsstkprice 2006.pdf.

Chapter 12

1. Major Garrett. "After the Wave: Mitch McConnell Wants to Learn from History, but His New Recruits Will Not Be Easily Led," *The National Journal*, October 23, 2010.
2. Ruthann Lariscy, *Why Negative Political Ads Work*, January 2, 2012, http://www.cnn.com/2012/01/02/opinion/lariscy-negative-ads/index.html.

References

Abrashoff, Michael, *It's Your Ship* (New York: Warner Books, 2002).

Babauta, Leo, *The Power of Less* (New York: Hyperion, 2009).

Bloom, Paul, *How Pleasure Works* (New York: W.W. Norton & Company, 2010).

Branden, Nathaniel, *How to Raise Your Self-Esteem* (New York: Bantam Books, 1988).

Bridges, William, *Transitions—Making Sense of Life's Changes* (Da Capo Press, 2004).

Buettner, Dan, *Thrive—Finding Happiness the Blue Zones Way* (National Geographic Society, 2010).

Burton, Robert. *On Being Certain-Believing You Are Right Even When You're Not* (St. Martin's Press, 2008).

Cozolino, Louis J., *The Neuroscience of Human Relationships, Attachment and the Developing Social Brain* (New York: W.W. Norton & Company, 2007).

Davidson, Martin, *The End of Diversity as We Know It* (San Francisco: Berrett-Koehler Publishers, 2011).

Doidge, Norman, *The Brain That Changes Itself* (New York: Penguin Group USA, 2008).

Dourado, Phil, *The 60 Second Leader* (New York: MJF Books, 2007).

Ferrazzi, Keith, *Never Eat Alone* (New York: Currency Doubleday, 2005).

Ferrazzi, Keith, *Who's Got Your Back—The Breakthrough Program to Build Deep, Trusting Relationships That Create Success—and Won't Let You Fail* (New York: Broadway Books, 2009).

Finkelstein, Sydney, *Why Smart Executives Fail* (New York: Portfolio, 2004).

Forni, P. M., *Choosing Civility: The Twenty-Five Rules of Considerate Conduct.* (New York, NY: St. Martin's Press, 2002).

Forni, P. M., *The Civility Solution: What to Do When People Are Rude* (New York: St. Martin's Press, 2008).

Gladwell, Malcolm, *Blink: The Power of Thinking Without Thinking* (New York: Little, Brown and Company, 2005).

Goldsmith, Marshall, *What Got You Here Won't Get You There* (New York: Hyperion, 2007).

Goleman, Daniel, *Emotional Intelligence: Why It Can Matter More Than IQ* (New York: Bantam, 2006).

Goleman, Daniel, *Primal Leadership: Learning to Lead With Emotional Intelligence* (Harvard Business Press, 2004).

Goleman, Daniel, *Working with Emotional Intelligence* (New York: Bantam, 1998).

Gonthier, Giovenella, and Morrissey, Kevin, *Rude Awakenings: Overcoming the Civility Crisis in the Workplace* (Chicago Dearborn Trade Publishing, 2002).

Gostick, Adrian, and Chester, Elton, *The Carrot Principle* (New York: Free Press, 2007).

Granger, Russell, *The 7 Triggers to Yes—The New Science Behind Influencing People's Decisions* (New York: McGraw-Hill, 2008).

Hacala, Sara, *Saving Civility* (Woodstock, VT: SkyLight Paths Publishing, 2011).

Hallowell, Edward, *Shine* (Boston: Harvard Business Review Press, 2011).

Heath, Chip, and Heath Dan, *Made to Stick* (New York: Random House, 2007).

Hsieh, Tony, *Delivering Happiness* (New York: Grand Central Pub, 2010).

Johnson, Thomas, *Relevance Regained* (New York, Toronto: Free Press Maxwell Macmillan, 1992).

Kabachnick, Terri, *I Quit But Forgot to Tell You* (Largo: The Kabachnick Group, Inc.)

Kotter, John and Whitehead, Lorna, *Buy* In—Saving Your Good Ideas from Getting Shot Down* (Harvard Business Review Press, 2010).

Kotter, John, and Heskett, James, *Corporate Culture and Performance* (New York: Free Press, 1992).

Kurzban, Robert, *Why Everyone (Else) Is a Hypocrite* (Princeton, NJ: Princeton University Press, 2010).

Lancaster, Lynne, *When Generations Collide* (New York: Harper Collins, 2002).

Loehr, Jim, and Schwartz, Tony, *The Power of Full Engagement* (New York: Free Press Paperbacks, 2003).

Mann, Tomas E., and Ornstein, Norman J., *It's Even Worse Than It Looks* (New York: Basic Books, 2012).

Marciano, Paul, *Carrots and Sticks Don't Work* (New York: McGraw-Hill Professional, 2011).

Marsh, Jason; Mendoza-Denton Rodolfo, and Smith, Jeremy, *Are We Born Racist?* (Boston: Beacon Press, 2010).

McCain, John with Salter, Mark. *Why Courage Matters* (Random House, 2004).

Medina, John, *Brain Rules* (Seattle, WA: Peer Press, 2008).

Miller, Marc, *A Seat at the Table* (Austin, TX: Greenleaf Book Group Press, 2009).

Moawad, Bob, and Hoisington, T. J., *The Secret of the Slight Edge* (New York: Aviva Publishing, 2007).

Olver, Kim, and Baugh, Sylvester, *Leveraging Diversity at Work* (Country Club Hills, IL: Inside Out Press, 2006).

Patterson, Kerry, Grenny, Joseph, McMillan, Ron, and Switzler, Al, *Crucial Conversations* (New York: McGraw-Hill, 2002.

Pink, Daniel, *Drive, The Surprising Truth About What Motivates Us* (New York: Riverhead Books, 2009).

Ramsey, Dave, *Entreleadership* (New York: Howard Books, 2011).

Rath, Tom, and Clifton, Donald, *How Full Is Your Bucket?* (New York: Gallup Pr, 2004).

Restak, Richard, *The Naked Brain* (New York: Three Rivers Press, 2006).

Roizen, Michael, and Oz, Mehmet, *You Being Beautiful: The Owner's Manual to Inner and Outer Beauty* (New York: Free Press, 2008).

Sanders, Tim, *The Likeability Factor* (New York: Three Rivers Press, 2006).

Schmidt, Ron, and Lent, John, *How Am I Treating You?* (Cleveland: Civility Press, 2009).

Schulz, Kathryn, *Being Wrong—Adventures in the Margin of Error* (HarperCollins, 2010).

Seligman, Martin, *What You Can Change and What You Can't* (Knopf, 1993).

Senge, Peter, *The Fifth Discipline* (New York: Currency Doubleday, 1990).

Siegel, Daniel J., *The Mindful Brain* (New York: W.W. Norton & Company, 2007).

Skinner, B. F., *Beyond Freedom and Dignity* (Indianapolis/Cambridge: Hackett Publishing Company, 1971).

Smith, David Livingstone, *Less Than Human* (New York: St. Martin's Griffin, 2011).

Szollose, Brad, *Liquid Leadership* (Austin, TX: Greenleaf Book Group, 2011).

Taylor, Lynn, *Tame Your Terrible Office Tyrant (TOT)!* (Hoboken, N.J: Wiley, 2009).

Thompson, Henry, *The Stress Effect* (San Francisco: Jossey-Bass, 2010).

Walters, Ronald, *Freedom Is Not Enough* (Lanham, MD: Rowman & Littlefield Publishers, 2007).

Washington, Denzel, *A Hand to Guide Me* (Des Moines, IA: Meredith Books, 2006).

Weiss, Joseph, *Organizational Behavior and Change* (Minneapolis/St. Paul: West Pub. Co., 1996).

West, Cornel, *Race Matters* (Boston: Beacon Press, 1993).

Whitney, John, *The Trust Factor* (New York: McGraw Hill, 1994).

Zak, Paul - *The Moral Molecule: The Source of Love and Prosperity.* (Dutton Adult, 2012).

Zukav, Gary, and Francis, Linda, *The Heart of the Soul—Emotional Awareness* (New York: Fireside, Simon & Schuster 2001).

Index

About the Author

Paul Meshanko is an author, internationally recognized speaker and business leader with over 20 years of experience in leadership development and organizational culture change. After a 12-year career with AlliedSignal, he opened Legacy Business Cultures in 1997 to serve corporations growing demand for change management and employee engagement training.

Under his leadership, the business has grown to become one of the most successful staff development and employee survey providers for companies of all sizes. Legacy's client list includes the Fortune 500 and many global organizations seeking to enrich their productivity while creating a dynamic environment for each employee's success.

As a presenter and facilitator, Paul has captivated over a quarter million leaders and business professionals on five continents. His training materials have been translated into over 25 languages and his newsletter is read by thousands of subscribers each month.

His clients have included The Cleveland Clinic, DuPont, Parker Hannifin, BASF, Progressive Insurance, MTD, Johnson Controls, Symantec, McGraw-Hill, Toyota, The U.S. EPA, and Ernst & Young. Always with an eye toward research and science, his speaking themes include organizational and personal resilience, work-life balance, neuroleadership, diversity, employee engagement and respectful work cultures.

Paul holds a bachelor of science degree in business administration from The Ohio State University and a master of business administration degree from Baldwin Wallace College. A dedicated husband and father, he has been an active member of the Human Resource Planning Society and served on the board of directors for the Boys & Girls Clubs of Cleveland. His first book, *Conversations on Success*, was released in May 2006.

In July of 2013, Paul with his wife, Kim and their two children relocated from Cleveland to Washington, DC to open a satellite office for Legacy Business Cultures.

"We will keep our headquarters in Cleveland and have now launched a presence in the beltway where Legacy has strong linkages with companies and organizations looking to incorporate our training into their workplaces," said Paul. "Our teams of partners and advisors on respect, resiliency, diversity and employee training will continue to serve our global clients with a new emphasis on the east coast of the United States."